Our daily bread

Mieczyslaw Malinski

Our daily bread

TRANSLATED BY FRANCIS McDONAGH

A CROSSROAD BOOK
THE SEABURY PRESS · NEW YORK

1979
The Seabury Press
815 Second Avenue, New York, N.Y. 10017

First published in German translation from the Polish original
in 1976 by Verlag Herder, Freiburg im Breisgau, Federal
Republic of Germany.
Copyright © Verlag Herder KG 1976

This translation copyright © Search Press Ltd. 1979

Printed in the United States of America

Library of Congress Catalog Card Number: 79-50664
ISBN: 0-8164-0439-9

Contents

December
Those who wait for their Lord   1

January
When they saw the star   13

February
A sense of God's presence   25

March
Meeting Jesus on the way of the cross   35

April
Why are you so sad?   47

May
The mother of my Lord   59

June
Faith is living in the light   73

July
He went away alone to pray   85

August
The measure of love   97

September
Hope transforms everything   109

October
Bear one another's burdens   121

November
You will find rest   133

Our daily bread

December

Those who wait for their Lord

1   YOUR TIME. Advent. The earth, touched by a light frost, shows traces of white. Fog. Still air, not the slightest breath of wind. The trees are bare, the branches like wires. A grey sky hangs low over the land. The cold is damp and penetrating. People move about like sleep-walkers.

You see all this as if from a distance. You are not present; inside you there is emptiness. Not even sadness, just numbness. Not even indifference, just an absence of feeling. You do what you have to do mechanically, you work, clear up a few things, chat — and are still amazed that you have the strength to do it. You do not feel faith or hope or love. You do not feel people. You do not feel God.

This is your Advent. Sometimes it coincides with the same time in the Church's year, but not always.

2   AND HE BEGAN TO TEMPT HIM. It happens when you least expect it — in the loudest din of pleasure or on the way home at night, in conversation with someone close to you or when you close the door of your room behind you: suddenly you begin to realize your loneliness.

Like a hand desperately trying to hold on to the rungs of a ladder . . .

Like someone drowning, who knows his feet will not touch bottom . . .

If only you then had the power to believe, 'I am not alone'.

3 I HAVE FOUND THE SILVER PIECE. Again and again the question of the meaning of life must worry you. What do I want? What am I waiting for? What do I want to achieve? Have I discovered values which I want never to deny, for which I am ready to give up everything?

Do not be surprised that you are never as peaceful as the person who has found this. No one can answer these questions except with his whole life.

4 WOE TO YOUR RICH. *You have received your consolation.* The better housing we have, the more we have to eat and to wear, the more clearly the question rises up before us: what is life for? We evade this question. We act as though we were totally claimed by our worries, preoccupied with all sorts of problems. We put the question off, to a day when we have a clear, calm head.

And it can happen that you succeed in this. The question stops tormenting you. The only questions left are somewhere even better to live, even better clothes and food.

5 THE KINGDOM OF HEAVEN IS LIKE A TREASURE HIDDEN IN A FIELD. Where is it that the world is full of sunshine, laughter, friendship, lightheartedness and health? In London they say it's New York; in New York, California. In California they say it's like that in Paris and Rome; and in Paris they say, and in Rome, that it's like that in London.

But somewhere there's a world full of happiness.

6 HE WENT AND HANGED HIMSELF. How should we live? By the principle of counting and calculating? Giving in abundance where it might pay off, breaking with those who are no more use to us, squeezing as much as possible out of everyone; never letting anything out in case someone makes use of it to get the better of us; praising those who are well away from us, never saying a good word about people who may possibly become our rivals, destroying them behind their backs before they become opponents. Like that?

7   AND THEY BROUGHT HIM A MAN WHO WAS POSSESSED.
What's the link that joins everything together for you? Sex,
money, advancement, praise?

What are you possessed, obsessed, by that makes you turn a
means into an end and treat a triviality as the essence and meaning
of life?

Do you know what it is?

8   I WILL COME. Looking out of the window, nervously glancing
at the clock, restlessly going up and down the room. Or having
a longing: waiting for someone, for something.

There are various forms of waiting — this open, impatient
waiting, and the sort that one hides but which weighs no less
heavy. Human life consists of periods of waiting.

Among the various forms of waiting there is one which is the
most important and common to all, waiting for God.

9   YOU WILL FIND REST. We are like moths bumping against
light bulbs at night. And the suffering Jesus, as naive artists
portray him, looks with questioning eyes upon the restlessness
of men.

When will we come to rest?

A crushed car. A human body lies by the side of the road.
Under the newspaper a face can be seen. What deep peace lies
on it. For the first time?

10   THE LIGHT CAME INTO THE WORLD. We live in half-tones,
half-shadows, shades of grey. Good deeds cover motives of
dubious worth, clear intentions are accompanied by secret subsi-
diary motives.

Prudence blurs into cowardice, self-sacrifice into calculation,
cleverness into cunning, truthfulness into malicious gossip,
relaxation into idleness, thrift into avarice, honesty into brutality,
justice into cruelty. And the shadow line pushes insensibly
forward, further forward. The colours become greyer and greyer,
we lose more and more of our sense of wrong: only when it

happens do we realize that a thing is wrong, and has been wrong for a long time.

Until somewhere near us a great good deed occurs, something like love and light, in which we see all the colours in their full strength and feel shame for our own greyness.

11 HE WITHDREW TO BE ALONE. Each of us is like a child going through the town. Lots of streets, hundreds of shop windows. In one there are radios and televisions, in another puppets, in a third sweets.

By the kerb stands the latest model of a car. A brightly-coloured poster is stuck on a fence. Sporting events are announced in large letters. But do you know why you went into the town and where you are going? Of course sport and cars are nice things, but haven't you lost sight of the goal?

Each if us is like a traveller. In the distance there is a snow-covered peak, somewhere the sound of a stream, on the slope in the middle of the wood a clearing. But haven't you lost your way?

OK, why shouldn't you want to find the stream, but are you really on the right path?

12 LET HIM TAKE UP HIS CROSS. Somewhere in the darkness of uncertainty there is still inside you a glimmer of hope that your skill in living and protecting yourself will preserve you from serious illnesses and a frail old age.

Somewhere in the darkness of uncertainty there is still inside you a glimmer of hope that your knowledge of the world will protect you against the harm people may try and do to you.

And although you are passing through a waterless waste, although you are spared nothing and given nothing — somewhere in the darkness of uncertainty there is still a glimmer of hope inside you.

13 TO OBTAIN ETERNAL LIFE. And when you've got everything neatly arranged, enough money, security, when you've worked yourself into a good position and want to start enjoying it, he will blow it all away. He will pull your glittering crown from your head and turn the riches into ash. You will stubbornly put the broken pieces together again, stick the paper crowns back in place, try to get back into the saddle — and when you have built your kingdom once more and begin to rule in it, he will destroy it for you again. And he will go on turning your sweetness into bitterness and your wealth into ash, he will make your plans dissolve into nothing. To make you realize.

14 AND PUT MY HAND INTO HIS SIDE. In a spotless white shirt, with manicured fingernails. Applauding — with one hand. A visitor to receptions, exhibitions, churches, theatres, an observer of human souls and their sufferings and joys. Untouched, unmoved. Indulgently looking at the people who have singed their wings in the fire like moths. Full of complacency that nothing like that has happened to you — that you haven't let yourself be taken in. With a conventional smile which neither you nor anyone else believes in. With apparent seriousness you talk about the weather and holidays. But you are not there at all: you are absent. They know too that you are not present. There is only a wall there, your contempt. But you sit in an ivory tower, concentrating on surviving the storms that whirl across your sky.

Really you are a child who has been hurt and feels insulted by people and the world, a child who cannot get over his hurt — and cannot forgive.

15 THE CHILDREN OF THIS WORLD. What are you good for any more? To come along when it's all over, shake someone's hand and say 'You were wonderful'?

We are spectators, tourists of life, who always take our places among the spectators, not in the ring. And our main rule is: Don't get involved in arguments, don't show your thoughts or intentions, not even by a smile or a flicker of the eyebrows, not by the slightest word. And watch them all having to go at one another. Then, when it's all over, when they've solved your problems with their hands when they start to carry out the bodies of

5

the heroes, then you will shake their hands as they pass, hang laurel wreaths around their necks and know at last what the right behaviour is.

You'll say that the picture is too harsh: they won't have to come and find us when there are great things to be done. We won't let them down then. But getting involved in nonsense, it's a waste of time and energy. It's just not worth risking one's own career for that. But be honest: these great things don't seem to happen much when you are around.

16   GIVE AN ACCOUNT OF YOUR STEWARDSHIP. You play differently when in what may be a very mediocre hand you spot a good card. The only problem is knowing how to play it. You don't want to have to give it up at the end of the game without having used it, through lack of skill, fear or carelessness.

Have you already played the trump in your life? If so, and if you succeeded with it, you will admit that life is easier for you now. The memory of that great moment casts a sparkle over the whole of the rest of life. It gives courage, generosity, a sense of worth.

But maybe for you the moment has yet to come. Look out, or at the end of your life you'll find that you still have the trump clenched in your hands. Until the moment when it's taken off you and thrown away.

17   AND CAME TO AN AGREEMENT WITH THEM. If you knew how much you have received and how much is still due to you, what you are responsible for and what doesn't affect you any more. If only you knew. But you don't. You don't know where tiredness ends and sloth begins, how much relaxation you need and where time-wasting starts. How much work you should take on and how much you should leave to your colleagues. How far the pangs of conscience go and where sick imagination begins. You keep on rushing this way and that, but you're never sure. And no one can free you from these doubts, ever.

18 ON THE WAY. You cannot wait until the last pieces of scaffolding drop away, the last holes, mountains of bricks, piles of sand and steel frameworks disappear — until your world is finally in order. You can't wait until you finally move in on your fifth floor and exercise your authority in peace.

No such world exists. In fact, whenever you place the next brick on your security you must already be thinking how you are going to remove it.

And you will die surrounded by piles of disordered things, amoung mountains of unfinished work, while you are busy constantly rebuilding your life.

19 WHILE YOU HAVE THE LIGHT. Listen to the sand running through your life-glass. How many more years? How many months? How many hours have you got left? Have you got a sense of time?

How do you live? How much of this time do you give to important things, to which you devote yourself, to which you are committed? Is there anything like that in your life? Perhaps your life is oozing away in emptiness, in some drivel or other. In eating. In dashing about. In some unimportant work. In some sort of relaxation and rest. Later the years will come — they're not far away — and you'll be busy looking after your collapsing organism. You'll be concentrating on medicines, medical techniques, on how to prolong your life, or rather your vegetable state, to increase the number of your empty days.

Listen to the sand running through your life-glass.

20 WHOEVER RECEIVES YOU RECEIVES ME. We have closed the doors of our homes and drawn the curtains. Broken with people and are stewing in our own juice. At best we stick to the same crowd, where everyone has known for years who knows what and who'll say what. We feel comfortable in this bulging armchair; we have a sense of our own value.

And you won't admit that you are afraid of worthwhile people because in their presence your deficiencies are revealed — in front of them you feel how inadequate you are in every way.

You avoid them because contact with them forces you to concentrate, to pay attention, to make an effort, demands work, change, renewal.

You are becoming dull. Because you have broken with people — with God, who wants to come to you in them.

21 ANYONE WHO LEADS ONE OF THESE LITTLE ONES ASTRAY. What do you want to give to the world? What mark do you want to leave on it? How are you going to educate your child or your field? To be a human being? To be an active, skilful human being, to be people who can look after themselves, who can work and behave properly. But what do these words mean for you? What philosophy of life is behind them? The philosophy of a person who is never satisfied, but is deliberately awkward to those who cross him — or that of a person who wants to do good?

You give the world what you are yourself. You cannot hide behind the curtain of your words. You bring up this child, or your friend, or the people you associate with, according to the measure of your personality.

22 IF YOU WILL WORSHIP ME. If only it were so easy to find out the address of one of the devils to whom people sell themselves! But the address is unobtainable. Not because there would be crowds outside the door, but because the devil has no fixed address. He is everywhere. And secondly, is he supposed to promise the same things to everyone, that they will have all the riches of the world? No one would believe him.

But the devil does give you things. He gives you a car — a better car. A job — a better job, a rise — a bigger rise, a holiday — a longer holiday, a reputation, a greater reputation. He gives you these things for the price of possession. If you say you want to obtain something at any price, you obtain it. But you must remember that, just as the cancerous tissue undermines the whole organism, this possession will devour your personality, block all the essential avenues of your development, destroy your vocation and your creative faculties. In future you will only be able to think of this one thing, concentrate on that, direct all your steps towards it, link your feelings with this one thing. And you will stop seeing anything else, stop reacting to anything else. You will be nothing more than a centre of rottenness which has settled into its prey. You will have what you wanted to have.

The most tragic thing is that in the course of time you will lose all power of self-criticism and no longer know what stage of possession you are in. Or how much of you is left, and what the cancer of possession has already eaten away.

23 THOSE WHO WAIT FOR THEIR LORD. The windows have been cleaned, the furniture dusted, the last of the washing done. You've got yourself a new winter coat, new shoes for the cold weather. The special joint is prepared. Everything is ready.

Now all you have to do is give the floor another wash and go to the hairdresser. That should be everything.

Someone looking from afar at our earth would be surprised by this fever of preparation, the trade swelling like an avalanche from day to day in the shops, this washing, baking and cleaning.

What are people making all these preparations for?

Who are they expecting?

24 THEY WENT BACK PRAISING GOD. Tidy up, polish, dust, cook, bake, sing Christmas carols, buy a Christmas tree, make paper garlands and decorations for the tree. Get some plywood and make a crib, little trees, a star and sheep, shepherds and kings. Mary. Joseph and the child. Sing Christmas carols. Decorate the tree, hang the garlands and tinsel on it, put candles on it. Sing Christmas carols. Write letters and cards to people you owe a sign of remembrance. Put the presents under the tree. Put on your best clothes. Sit down at the table with your loved ones.

Sing Christmas carols in front of the crib, round the Christmas tree, in church. So that your dark interior finally becomes bright with the light. So that your deaf ears finally hear the voice. So that Jesus is born in your heart.

25 I WILL STAY WITH YOU. Your holidays. It is like it was in the past, when you were a child. In your Sunday suit, which hurt you a bit because it was still too new, you went up to the door, turned the handle and slowly and with a secret excitement opened the door. Through the crack you could see the table with the Christmas tree on it, with the candles, the shining foil and the glittering globes. For fear that you might scare away this mystery you tiptoed in among the decorations and shining furniture.

The only change since that time is that you have grown big and crude, have become less sensitive. Everything else has stayed just the same. The same ceremonies, customs, gestures, pictures, words, songs — the reflection of a reality concealed behind them.

Approach your festivals as you used to when you were a child — filled with awe, on tiptoe, and let the mystery reveal itself to you from behind its symbols.

26 THE TIME CAME FOR HER DELIVERY, AND SHE BORE HER SON. It is not enough to wish all the best, every happiness, to hope that the parents will be able to be proud of their children and that the children will have rich parents. It is not enough to have the Christmas table with the crib, the Christmas tree and the carols.

We cannot escape the nagging knowledge that this is not what it's about, that all this only symbolizes a reality which is as tangible as the crib and yet as elusive as memory. We are left with the uncomfortable feeling that this reality could pass us by, that we could somehow become poorer if we don't come in contact with it.

Or perhaps we persuade ourselves and others that no mysteries of that sort exist and that the only reality consists in these bright globes on the Christmas tree, in the decorations, the best clothes and the special meal.

27 THEY CAME IN HASTE. It is us who look for the star and make all speed to the cave in Bethlehem. We want to see with our own eyes, to hear with our own ears, to feel with our own hands. To convince ourselves that this silent, awe-inspiring vault of heaven, that this painful human fate of ours, that all of it has a meaning. To reassure ourselves that what we so much want to believe in, what we try to live for, is not a deception.

To see it with our own eyes, to hear it with our own ears, to feel it with our own hands, this sign of our hope.

28 WE ANNOUNCE TO YOU A GREAT JOY. The further the years recede from us, the more we need the story of the son of man born in a stable and laid in the manger because there was no room for him in the inn.

The more the years fly from our reach, the further the angels, the stars, the brightness and the candles on the Christmas tree slip from our sight — and all that is left is he who was born in the stable and failed in his life, who was abandoned by his friends in the hour of trial and ended up on the cross.

The further the years flow from us, the more we need this story, to hear a confirmation of our efforts, which so often remain unsuccessful, to recover the meaning of our lives.

29 AND SAW A LIGHT. In the days that get shorter and shorter, in your days, in the years that get shorter and shorter and colder and colder — you have a light. In your despondency, in your revulsion from people who are so hard, selfish and indifferent, in all the dreariness which daily becomes greater in you — he is your light. He is the proof that a person can be great, selfless, good, kind and loving.

In your resignation to yourself, which grows with the years, in the conviction that all you are good for is selfishness, he is your hope that you can stir yourself to do great and good things.

As our years grow darker and colder we need his light all the more in order to be able to go on living as human beings.

30 THEY FELL DOWN AND WORSHIPPED HIM. Light the candles on the Christmas tree, spread out the cards underneath it, put on a record of Christmas carols, forget that outside the window it's all dark and frosty. Let your eyes linger on the glitter of the tree,

11

on the light and colours, and travel with Mary and Joseph to Bethlehem, come with the shepherds to Mary, Joseph and the child, search for the holy family with the three wise men and — as you did in the past when you were a child — believe like a child that love is possible, and loyalty, and sacrifice and unselfishness.

In a minute you'll have to get up, put out the lights and go out into the darkness and frost.

31 AND YOU WILL SEE THE SON OF MAN COMING ON THE CLOUDS OF HEAVEN. Another year gone.

Don't just say 'over and done with'. There was a lot of good in it, quite definitely good. It was not just a step in time, it was your step on the way to God. So much love, so many attempts to overcome your own egoism.

Perhaps you'll say, 'It hurts me to hear you say that. I can't see any of this good.'

Have a look. So much getting up early in the morning, so much hurrying so as not to be late, so many hours' honest work, so much honesty, help at home, so much care. Yes, so much love.

God is infinitely just. That means above all that he does not forget the least good deed, not the simplest word, not the smallest kind thought.

When they saw the star

1   HE CAME TO HIS OWN. We who live on specks of the universe, a universe which is so vast that our minds are just unable to comprehend it — we believe that its creator has noticed us. We, who belong to that species called humanity, which in the life of the universe occupies no more than the twinkling of an eye — we believe that its creator has noticed us and given us a sign — his son.

2   LET IT BE TO YOU ACCORDING TO YOUR FAITH. In the stable there were no angels. There were angels, but they were with the shepherds who kept watch.

A star led the three wise men, but in the place where the child was no miracles took place.

Soon after the son of God was in flight from the jealous puppet ruler of the little state. After that came thirty years' work as a carpenter in some out-of-the-way place and barely a couple of years' public activity when he worked miracles, no differently from the prophets and God's chosen representatives in the Old Testament.

No one can force a person to believe and love, even if God himself were to ask for this faith and love.

3   WHEN THEY SAW THE STAR. You won't see the star of Bethlehem unless you look for it. You won't hear the angels'

song unless you make an effort.

And who needs to watch for consolation more than us, appalled as we are by the diseases which flourish so near to us, by the death which circles round us, by all the unhappiness which shatters the life we have so painfully got straight, by the old age into which we all gradually decline?

And who needs more to listen to saving voices than us, as we become more and more aware of our clumsiness, our weakness, our frailty, our malice, and not least of our stupidity, as we become gradually more depressed and unhappy?

You won't find the star of redemption unless you look for it. You won't hear the words of truth unless you yearn for them.

4 NOTHING IS IMPOSSIBLE. Tonight the wolf offers his paw, foxes eat from one's hand, tigers curl up like cats; lions stretch out their necks to be scratched, snakes twinkle their eyes, scorpions smile, hens stop cackling. Even the monkey opposite speaks with a human voice.

And even though in the morning the miracle is over and life returns to normal, don't forget that a miracle is possible and people can be human beings. You too can be a human being.

5 SHE LAID HIM IN A MANGER. How can we not want possessions when others have them? How can we not want more when others have more? How can we not want a better life when others have a better life? This is the way material things block your imagination, your mind and your feelings. From that point you no longer hear anything. You no longer see anything, no longer feel anything. Your hands will now only brush the hard surface of a thing. Then you're caught. Anyone can have you if he just slips you something, if he just throws money on the table. You are no longer free. You are no longer free, but just a collector obsessed by the lust for possessions.

That is why Jesus is always telling us that we must be, but not want to have, that we must do, but not accumulate things, that we must give, but not acquire. That is why he was born in an inn and laid in a manger.

6 AND THEY OFFERED HIM GIFTS, GOLD, FRANKINCENSE AND MYRRH. This is the only way we can approach God — with gold, incense and myrrh: with the gold of a love which extends to complete surrender, complete sacrifice, with the incense of unending fascination, with the myrrh of suffering, sadness and a sense of sin.

   This is the only way we can approach God — the only way we can approach ourselves, ourselves as tiny beings confronted with the immenseness of reality, to which we penetrate through love, fascination and suffering.

7 THREE WISE MEN. What do you think? Do you think? How much is what you call your thinking moulded by the world which surrounds you, by school, newspapers, radio, television, books, talks? How much is your thinking influenced by your moods, passions, obsessions and fears, influenced by what you want at any price to have or avoid? How far are you free to think, to judge, to give an opinion, to find explanations, to look for new ways and solutions.

   Ultimately, of course, you are a wise man, you seek the truth. You must never give up the search, because God is truth. If you give up truth you give up God.

8 IN HIS IMAGE AND LIKENESS. Stay as God created you, with your totally unrepeatable reactions, feelings and thoughts. Don't let yourself be brought into line by society. Don't let yourself be made to conform with the group in which you live.

   Don't let yourself be reduced to uniformity by the pressure of the group in which you live. You'll manage it, but only if you demand a great deal from yourself, if you keep trying to improve.

   Have respect for the person beside you. Let him develop. Don't want to make him like you. Don't envy the fact that he has kept his naturalness.

9 LIKE CHILDREN. These years that lie behind you, what have they left of your simplicity, genuineness and spontaneity? Are

you still capable of being ashamed, pleased, fascinated, enraptured, amazed? Or perhaps you are ashamed of your feelings: after so many years of life one really ought to know that the only thing that counts is what brings in money, one should only get involved in things which are safe and without danger.

10   FOLLOW ME. Be like a river. Don't try to be like a monument. Don't save up those of your ideas, sayings and features which have proved themselves, which you are sure suit you, which have found a response in your surroundings. Don't even save up your convictions, your views, your judgments. Be like a river. That is harder. It's easier to bring out of your storehouse a prepared smile, clever phrases and answers, obvious ideas. But then you don't even notice that you have become a piece of dead wood.

Be like a river. That is harder. Almost dangerous. The fear that an answer, a solution or an idea won't come to you in time, so that you'll have to go into the dark and keep having to search afresh. That's harder, but only then are you a human being, a green branch and not a piece of dead, black wood.

11   YOU ARE LIKE WHITED SEPULCHRES. Who are you really? Perhaps even you don't know because you hide from yourself behind the smokescreen of your tricks and twists and turns. Because you hide your real face from yourself behind the banner of a pose and a pretence.

You must look at yourself. For the sake of your humanity, your redemption. Look at yourself, even if you seem to be a bottomless void; even if you see yourself as a pit full of malice, falsehood and untruth. And don't give up, but fight for the truth in your life, so that your action, your word, represents what is in you.

12   BROOD OF VIPERS. Don't be a chameleon, changing to match your surroundings. Don't be an octopus, grabbing everything which comes within reach of your arms and not letting it go until you've sucked it dry. Don't be a peacock and spread your feathers

before everyone. Don't be a jackal, slinking around old people. Be a human being. A creature that gives advice, helps, is obliging, tells someone else the truth to his face, forgives before being asked to.

Then you will be — even if no one asks you whether you believe and who you believe in — a star leading to God, the Father of light.

13 WHO ARE YOU? As far as possible, get everything done straight away. Don't delay necessary conversations. Don't put it off when you have to clarify your position or make an important decision. Sooner or later you will be in a position where you have to do it, which will be even worse for you than this one.

Try to express yourself clearly and completely. Avoid half-tones, half-light. Avoid ambiguity or persistent vagueness. Otherwise unclarity and disorder will pile up to the extent that even you won't know any longer who you are and who the people around you are. Then life will become unbearable.

14 WHOEVER SEEKS TO SAVE HIS LIFE WILL LOSE IT. Don't be hypnotized by yourself, by your past or your future, by your successes or your defeats, by your youth or your old age; your wild fear and despair will paralyze you. You must get out of the closed circle of your own self through commitment, sacrifice, love, trust and faith.

This is the way of true artists, true parents, true politicians, true Christians — true human beings.

15 WHEN YOU ARE OLD. You can't march in the same uniform all your life. You can't act like a child when you aren't one any more. You can't go around like a schoolboy when you're a student or like a student when you're working for yourself; you can't behave like an ordinary employee when you're supposed to lead, or like a bachelor when you're married. Your functions change, and your duties, rights and responsibilities. Your life changes and so do you. You must make a new start, even if

sometimes you have no desire to abandon your previous position. Otherwise you'll bring a great deal of trouble on yourself and others — and you'll be ridiculous.

16 AND LEAD US NOT INTO TEMPTATION. Never say it's too late. It's never too late, no matter what marvellous opportunity you've missed, what great mistake you've made, what tragic situation you're in, or however old you are.

It can always be too late, even when you're first at the start, even when you have the best starting position, even when all the possibilities are open to you, even when you are very young.

Everything depends on you, on your trust — in yourself, in people, in the world, in God.

17 IN SECRET. You will only find out what someone is worth when a gap appears in the normal course of events, when there is a chance of getting something at the cost of some dishonesty and all the signs are that no one will ever find out.

Only then, when you find yourself placed in a situation of that sort, will you be able to be sure what you are worth.

18 BLESSED ARE THOSE WHO MOURN, FOR THEY SHALL BE COMFORTED. Do not wait for a time when your moment will come and your work finally be justly valued, your intentions understood and your efforts recognized. Don't wait to convince your opponents and secure the praise your life deserves. Even when it happens, the next day someone will appear who is better than you, more interesting, more original or harder-working, more self-sacrificing, more committed, someone who draws all attention to himself and entices your followers away from you, while you go back into the shadow.

19 WHOEVER WANTS TO BE THE GREATEST. Being human. There were so many nice boys and girls; they have grown into unpleasant young contemporaries.

There were so many hopeful young people; soon they began to do nothing but make money. So many beautiful boy friends and girl friends; they became unbearable as soon as they got top jobs. There were so many upright husbands and virtuous wives; in their later years they became Philistines, play-actors, unrestrained sensualists.

Being human, being Christian.

20 WE SAW HIS STAR. And you thought you were too old to want to get involved in the uncertain adventure of someone else's worries.

And you thought you were too cynical to get enthusiastic about someone or win someone's affection.

And you thought you had too much experience for anything else to be capable of arousing your wonder or interest.

You were too companionable to cut yourself off from your gang of friends — just for the sake of a person in trouble.

You were too calculating to put your own interests last and help someone to look for a lost silver piece.

You thought everything that could happen in your life had already happened and nothing else could stop you cultivating your own patch.

But now perhaps you're not at all sorry that — maybe for the last time in your life — you have a chance to find out the meaning of your life and become enthusiastic about the good, the true and the beautiful — for God himself.

21 WHOEVER WANTS TO BE MY DISCIPLE. The paths of great men and women look to us like straight clear roads. That depresses us, especially when we look at our own lives, which are full of wrong turnings, full of defeats, attempts to go back, full of blind alleys.

The paths of great men and women look to us like bright sunshine. That is an illusion. If we look closely at their paths, they are full of wrong turnings, defeats, attempts to go back, full of blind alleys.

Only they have more patience than us in getting up from a fall, more persistence in the search for the right model, more consistency in striving for hidden goals.

22 MEN OF VIOLENCE. If only one could repeat one's life. If only one could get back just a year, just a month, just a day, just an hour. If one could unsay a word, undo a deed.

And yet. Don't try to live too carefully. Don't devote too much energy to rubbing out your mistakes. Do something in your life. Only if you tackle a thing with go, with spirit, will you obliterate what is called sin, mistake, wrong. There just won't be any time for it. And again, make allowance for a risk: here and there you may be unsuccessful, you may upset some people or get in their way. That will be incomparable with the good you bring about. That will make up for all your mistakes.

23 YOUR CARE MUST BE FOR THE KINGDOM OF GOD. When we look for reasons why religious life has lost its attraction, one very plausible one is perhaps that we are not alone in the world. We constantly come up against other people; it gives us a feeling of security. We soothe ourselves with the thought that other people manage to live somehow; with the inevitability of death before their eyes, they still do not despair, they do not go mad with the fear of having to answer for their wrong-doing. They seem to have sorted out the problems that worry us. Another reason. We are not confronted with an alien nature, but with a cultivated world, that is, with a nature transformed by man. We are no longer so afraid of lightning, drought and flood.

Maybe one day the cars on the roads will be steered automatically, and you won't need to be afraid that there might be an accident. We may learn to make rain and drive away clouds. We may find cures for heart attacks, cancer and sclerosis. Then it will be even harder for us to be religious.

But in the last resort man in all ages is poor. In the last resort there is always a new danger, a new ailment, lurking. There is always the endless line of death, meaninglessness and grief.

20

24 HE WAS AFRAID AND BEGAN TO SINK. We are going along the narrow strip of normality and habit. Under our feet yawn the pits of oblivion. To right and left we are pressed in by the slippery walls of loathing and disgust. Above our heads there is dizzying black space, in the distance the clouds of lowering fears. You are going along the deceptive surface of normality. Only a step and you'll plunge into the chasm of apathy, be overwhelmed by prejudices and complexes, be swallowed up by fear and anxiety. Only a step and you'll stop seeing the world objectively, hearing what people say to you, stop thinking logically. You are going along the narrow strip of normality. Think about it. Learn to appreciate it.

25 ONLY THROUGH PRAYER AND FASTING. What does it mean to be normal or not to be normal? How many inherited burdens and complexes are inside us, acquired without our choice, and how many through our own fault, our stupidity, weakness, helplessness — and lastly, how many through our malice?

There is so much repressed anger in us, so much bitterness, envy, disgust and contempt. So much sadness, fear, inhibition, prejudice, presumption, irritation, lust for conquest, brutality, violence, crudeness, lack of control. So much suspicion, lying, deception and cunning.

How far are you normal? How far are you not normal? How much in you is inherited from your ancestors, how much derives from deep internal wounds from your childhood — and how much from your own fault?

What have you made of yourself? What are you making of yourself?

26 ONE WILL BETRAY ME. Don't say you didn't get on in your job because of your honesty, that you earned so little because your convictions wouldn't let you give or take a bribe, because you can't get in with your boss — because you can't do what so many people, those people, do.

When you talk like that you're already on the edge of betrayal.

27   OF LITTLE FAITH. Don't hide behind your meaninglessness, behind the wrong you have done in your life.

Don't hide behind your disorganization, your laziness, your lack of intelligence — behind all the faults you know about.

Don't be afraid of the people who are in your way or maliciously put obstacles in front of you. Don't be afraid if the world is difficult.

You have enough strength to do what you have to do. You get it from him who asks greatness of you.

28   I CAME TO CAST FIRE ON THE EARTH. Don't store up rage in yourself at other people. Don't keep coming back to the evil you have suffered. Don't keep staring, after sleepless nights, with growing indignation at the wrong people have done you. That hatred will narrow your horizon, will grow like a hump, will bend you, distort you, destroy you. It will make you hysterical and tear you to pieces. And only you will be responsible for your state.

You must lay this wrong at God's feet — as someone throws away a useless burden at the side of the road — and go on.

29   HE RAN TO MEET HIM. Don't try to talk yourself out of it by saying you will only go to him when you are worthy of him, when you have freed yourself of your bad habits, when you have mastered your faults, when the problems in your life are solved. Don't seek to convert yourself — your life isn't long enough. And anyway, that's not what he wants of you. He doesn't even ask for a first step; it's enough if you shyly lift up your head.

30   THE PHARISEE STOOD UPRIGHT. There is no situation which cannot be altered. No goal which requires everything to be fixed and secure. There is no perfect state. No final shape, no ideal form. Everything is a stage, at the end of which we must immediately go on, or else we lose any sort of present and find ourselves in the ridiculous situation of the complacent Pharisee.

It's the same with everything: with scientific and technical progress, with politics, culture and with personal development.

22

That's why when you come to die you should not feel sorry that you were unable to do so many things, that you were unable to live your time to the full, that you could not have years of peace and stability. They don't exist here.

You will find them there.

31   PLEASE. God, make us unsettled, dissatisfied with ourselves; make us look for you. So may it be. But, please, give us a little happiness, the happiness of the merchant when he found the coveted pearl, of the woman who found the silver piece; something of the happiness of the lost son who went home to his father.

February

A sense of God's presence

AND HE RETURNED TO NAZARETH. Scripture says almost nothing about Jesus' thirty years' residence in Nazareth, since in that time there was just nothing special happening. It was a quite ordinary life in a small town. Ordinary sunrises and sunsets, ordinary waking up. Ordinary prayers, meals, jobs and hours of relaxation. Ordinary springs, summers, autumns and winters. There were the mother, the father, the son, the neighbours, the people among whom Joseph the carpenter worked with his son Jesus.

They were thirty ordinary years. What was the point of them? To make us believe in the value an ordinary human life has in the sight of God.

1 WHO DO YOU SAY THAT I AM? Who do you say that I am? Jesus' question has confronted men for two thousand years. The question confronts each of us. And don't get out of it by saying that some say he's a prophet and others say something else. He is asking you: who do *you* say that I am?

2 TO ONE HE GAVE FIVE TALENTS, TO ANOTHER TWO. Not all became apostles. Only those to whom Jesus had said, 'Follow me'. Not all the women who were public sinners changed their way of life, only the one to whom Jesus had said, 'Your sins are forgiven. Go and sin no more'. Not all the publicans gave

25

up their profession, only the one to whom Jesus had said, 'Zacchaeus, make haste and come down; for I must stay at your house today'.

St John's way was different, and so was that of St Peter, and that of Nicodemus, and Veronica's and Mary Magdalen's . . .

Not all the people who are alive today are Christians. Not all Christians zealously fulfil their ecclesiastical duties. Not all those who zealously fulfil them are religious.

Everyone has his way, marked out for him by grace.

The most important thing is that a person, even one as perfect as the young man in the Gospel, does not refuse to follow his grace.

4 HE WHO HAS EARS, LET HIM HEAR. The Gospel is all the time talking about you.

You are the careless son who squanders his substance, the imprudent servant who buries his treasure, the selfrighteous Pharisee, the cleansed leper who does not think to give thanks for the grace of healing, Peter, who denies Jesus out of fear, Judas, who betrays him.

But you are also the blind man who comes into the road and cries, 'Jesus, son of David, have pity on me', Zacchaeus, to whom Jesus comes as a guest, Magdalen, who weeps at Jesus' feet, Matthew, who leaves everything where it is and follows Jesus, the faithful John, who sticks it to the final moment under the cross, Jesus, who goes about the earth doing good.

5 BE PERFECT. What has your desire for greatness led you to do? Where did you get the strength to clash with other people? Did you dismiss the clashes by saying, 'They're all stupid!? Or the reverse; when they showed you you were weak, did you get out to collect money, titles, positions, to acquire more comfort, more possessions?

The truth is that God created each of us as a unique, distinct human being whom no one else can threaten.

The truth is that we are all children of the same Father. And only when we grow into our surroundings and open ourselves to them can we fully develop our individuality.

6 A REED SWAYING IN THE WIND. We were carefully brought up from childhood. We were put in a line, rapped on the knuckles, stood in the corner, given sweets as a reward; our hair was cut so that the wind wouldn't mess it. We always had to watch ourselves to see that we weren't sweating, weren't catching cold, that nothing was doing us harm. We learned not to stick our fingers in doors, not to expose ourselves to any danger, not to take any risks. And already we've begun to be pleased that we're sensible, controlled and cold-blooded, that we're people who don't burst out.

How now are we supposed to have a desire for the water of life, how are we supposed to go out into the dark night to seek the truth, how are we to snatch the torches from the fire with our bare hands, how are we to work to the last drop of sweat — how now are we to commit ourselves totally?

7 DO NOT SAY. Do not assume that you *are* a student or an artist, a wife, a professor, a priest, a director. Do not assume you are a Catholic. Do not assume you are a human being. That is not just your state; it is principally a summons. You are *becoming* a student, a husband, an actor, a religious, an engineer. You are becoming a Catholic, you are becoming a human being — with every action. Or you betray your state with every action.

8 THEY SET OUT. People know you already: your failings and your strengths, your quirks and your weaknesses — people have already sorted out what sort of person you are. And in the end you realize too that you move in the fixed grooves of your possibilities. You even begin to get used to this pattern, you find that you manage comfortably with it.

You only come alive when that doesn't satisfy you, when you aren't satisfied with being sorted out in this way, when you are convinced that you are capable of more, that you haven't yet said your last word.

9   WHO TAKE THE KINGDOM OF HEAVEN BY FORCE. There's always the danger that we will adopt a nice, well adapted personality, which politely says 'Hello', 'Goodbye', and 'Excuse me', the type that confesses to missing its daily prayer or having bad thoughts, the sort that is terrified of itself, other people and the world, afraid of high-flying thoughts, great enthusiasm, great anger, that fears independent thought, independent moves or actions.

People like that do not decide to follow Jesus, no matter what stars appear to them, no matter what angels sing to them. They remain prudently calculating little people, ready to do down anyone who threatens to grow beyond their reach, for their peace and balance is more important to them than anything. And the worst thing is that they will do all this in the name of Jesus Christ, without grasping anything of his greatness.

10 TO EVERY ONE THAT HAS WILL MORE BE GIVEN. Do not excuse yourself with other people's behaviour. Don't hide behind their actions. Avoid justifications for your actions such as, 'If he doesn't bother about it, why should I do it?' or 'If they can do it, why can't I?' We shall be judged individually, since we receive an individual measure. When you look properly, you will find that you are the one that has received more.

Never compare yourself with other people. You don't know how much they have received. You only know how much you have received, and you are responsible for that.

11 IN THIS HOUR. Do not bow to the pressure of the moment. Do not allow yourself to try to obtain something at any price *now*, as though a vacuum would follow. Now is always followed by tomorrow, and you will have to look into the eyes of those whom only yesterday you wanted to dazzle, conquer or convince, from whom you wanted to get or wheedle small or great things. Time mercilessly reveals the motives of your actions — the slightest falsehood, the slightest deception — and brings the truth to light.

12 BY THE MEASURE WITH WHICH YOU MEASURE SHALL IT BE MEASURED TO YOU. You have the life you want to have. You have the life you are. There is no action which will go unpunished. All of them are left behind in you. Every decision forms further action. Every decision is a new trait in your personality. It remains now and for ever.

13 MY HOUR. The present moment is the intersection of two lines of force, the whole past — all our previous actions — and a present act of the will.

That is why we cannot say that this decision is just a result of the past, and why we also cannot say that it is totally free of the past.

But we can — at every moment — intervene in our lives by an act of will.

14 THE MOTHER OF JESUS SAID TO HIM. Go on, tell yourself once and for all that you don't want to win verbal duels. Don't try to establish your case with flashy phrases. Trust in the humanity of the person you are talking to. Have faith that words last longer than the moment in which they are uttered, that the other person will still sometimes come back to them, that they will sometimes still examine your arguments and their own.

And when you talk about God only say what you really believe. Don't cover an inner emptiness with big words; nothing can conceal it. The WORD OF GOD can only be effective when it comes from faith.

And when you talk about God don't make propaganda, don't misuse the WORD. Don't try to convert everyone at all costs. You have no power over the WORD. Conversion is not your work.

15 HYPOCRITES. Watch yourself when you say 'Hello' and 'How are you?', when you shake hands, nod and smile. Watch yourself when you tell the same joke for the umpteenth time, the same incident or adventure, when you talk about your discoveries, inventions or insights, about the grace you have received.

Watch yourself when you make the sign of the cross for the umpteenth time, when you pray, when you take part in the mass, when you receive communion.

So that you don't store up clichés and just keep on wheeling them out. So that you stay alive.

16 YOU ARE THE SALT OF THE EARTH. If you knew what people are saying about you. How they distort and twist your words and actions. How they attribute actions and words to you. The amount of slander, gossip, the number of rumours, malicious remarks and ironic jokes going round about you. Sometimes this wave of envy reaches you. Only then do you feel how you are surrounded by spying glances, by whispering, by fingers pointed at you. Then you're surprised that the people in the street still bother to return your greeting, that they still shake hands with you. And the more you work, the more you commit and give yourself, the worse things they will say about you — that is the price of a rich life.

But couldn't things be different? They can. Just live quite unobtrusively; don't make yourself unpopular with anyone. People will praise you, agree with you, greet you. Only then don't start thinking you're a Christian.

17 NOTHING IS COVERED THAT WILL NOT BE REVEALED. Don't look for excuses. Don't say it's untruth, slander, rumour, you didn't say it or do it, it wasn't like that. Don't try to explain that you didn't mean it, you had quite different intentions, you weren't understood, it's a case of misunderstanding.

Look, people are closing their windows already because they don't want to listen to any more of your whining explanations. Even your friend is only listening to you with half an ear, and someone else is absentmindedly inspecting his fingernails.

Don't make a thing about having to explain everything to them because truth or your good name or your honour is at stake. Drop it. Realize that the most important thing is what God thinks of you. Carry on doing your thing.

30

18 NO ONE WHO PUTS HIS HAND TO THE PLOUGH AND LOOKS BACK IS FIT FOR THE KINGDOM OF GOD. Don't keep on insisting on your rights. Don't make the excuse that you only want justice — you'll only get involved in hopeless arguments.

Don't look for revenge — not just because of loving your neighbour, but first of all for your own sake. It's a waste of you, of your energy, your time. Let it go. Do your work, your duty.

19 HE CALLED TO HIMSELF THOSE WHOM HE DESIRED. Don't imagine that your name is constantly on the lips of your acquaintances. It's not true that the bosses are constantly discussing you. Don't fool yourself that other people find you that interesting.

Usually what happens is that people don't see you. You don't exist for them. Those who need you become aware of you fleetingly. From time to time those who don't like you notice you.

You exist only for your friends, and even then only to a limited extent. Though even that is a great deal.

20 IF YOUR RIGHTEOUSNESS IS NOT GREATER THAN THAT OF THE PHARISEES. Don't chatter so much. Don't go on about what you think, what you believe in, what you'd like to have done by now, what plans and intentions you have, what hopes, perspectives and chances, what you disagree with, what you won't have, what you don't want, what you protest against, — all in the constant fear that someone might miss something important about you, in the constant fear that others might put you in the shade. Don't talk so much. Be quiet, or you'll be like an empty market-place with the wind blowing the rubbish over it. Calm down, so that you can come to yourself, find yourself.

21 I AM THE LIFE. Beware of the person who begins by saying 'I don't care about anything. Nothing affects me any more. I'm not bothered about anything'.

Beware of yourself when you begin by saying, 'I don't care about anything. Nothing affects me any more. I'm not bothered about anything'.

When you see that all the positions are occupied and all the roads are barricaded, that you have no future — don't stay alone in your room. Don't make any decisions. Go out into the world, among people or to church — to look for the life that has flowed out of you.

22 WOE TO YOU. Does your vocabulary include the threat 'Woe to you!'? Not for times when someone has done you an injury or trod on your corns, but for times when you see something wrong, injustice, deception, contempt for work and people, when you take someone else's injury, someone else's failure, someone else's defeat, to heart, when you can't bear someone else's humiliation or contempt.

Do you use the threat 'Woe to you!'? Or have you stopped?

23 GIVE TO HIM WHO ASKS. First of all you must be a human being, and only then can you be a civil servant, a worker, a teacher, priest or doctor. Your job may be important, even distinguished, but it still must not choke your humanity. The institution in which you work may be large, important, even holy, but you must not become its tool. If you keep slavishly to its rules you destroy people instead of serving them. None of them can relieve you of your responsibility for acting like a human being.

24 HE DROVE THEM ALL OUT OF THE TEMPLE. When dishonesty enrages you, don't just shrug your shoulders resignedly, but thump the table and protest. When you disagree with what people say to you, don't make a polite face, but say what you think about it. When you see that someone is not being honest, don't smile ironically — tell them straight out, whoever it is, your friend, your boss, your bishop.

You think people won't be very keen on it, and it will make

difficulties for you? You're probably right. You don't want to do it? It's up to you. Just give that sort of attitude its proper name, and admit to yourself that it's cowardice; don't try to disguise it as Christian love.

25 GET THEE BEHIND ME, SATAN. The translators of the Gospel have made many different attempts to interpret this passage, but they keep coming back to this curse, 'Get away from me, Satan' — Jesus' words to his first disciple, who was to be the rock of the Church. Peter only wanted the best for him. He wanted to save him from pain and death on the cross. He wanted him to be able to go on wandering through Palestine, enjoying the morning cool and the summer heat, to go on preaching the marvellous doctrine of the love of God and neighbour. After all, that was what people needed so much.

Are you a Christian? Are you ready to say the same thing to those who want to keep you back, so that you don't go too far, and show you a comfortable slot? Are you ready to say the same thing to yourself when the temptation to comfort and opportunism springs up in you?

26 AND HE BEGAN TO TREMBLE. Every human being is afraid of himself or herself, not just you. Even the cleverest, even the most self-assured, even the most beautiful — they all know they have weaknesses.

Everyone is afraid of showing himself up, not just you.

And everyone, not just you, is faced with the task of breaking out of his own stupidity, of conquering his own shyness and cowardice. Even when you think you can never understand that, that you'll never learn it.

27 BLESSED ARE THE PEACEMAKERS. You fear superiors, colleagues, people in the street, you fear that they will discover your ignorance, your weakness, your perplexity, your feel that they'll make you a laughing stock and get power over you. That's the reason for that defensive attitude, stiff and unnatural, the attempt

to seem cleverer and stronger, the reason for the attack to antici-
pate aggression, the gruffness, the irony, the destruction of a rival
in their absence — with a rumour, slander and calumny.

But you must realize that they fear you too. They are afraid
that you will discover their intellectual failings, their physical
weaknesses and their ridiculous features. That's the reason for
their artificial expressions, the severity, the irony, the intrigues.

Why agonize? Try to take other people into your confidence.
Convince them that you don't intend to do them an injury, that
you are well disposed towards them. Be kind to them!

28 BEAR ONE ANOTHER'S BURDENS. Even when it's hard for
you to get used to, you must accept it. There aren't only people
that you can't stand, but also those who don't like you. There
are not just people around you whom you regard as shallow and
superficial; others have a similar view of you. Not only do you
know people who put you off; there are also those who find you
unbearable. You are not the only one who can point to people
you think immoral; there are also those who are firmly convinced
that you are dishonest.

And the saddest thing is that they're at least partly right.

March

Meeting Jesus on the way of the cross

1 CRUCIFY HIM. Jesus' sacrifice is his life. A life in freedom. The life of a man who succeeded in freeing himself from internal compulsions and outward pressure, who thought, spoke and acted in accordance with his conscience. He saw faults and distortions and stood up for man in the name of truth and RIGHTEOUS-NESS. Jesus' cross is simply the consequence of such a life.

2 CONFESSING THE CRUCIFIED. We confess Jesus Christ — this man who was crucified.

If that's true, don't be surprised that the good Lord doesn't send crowds of angels to help you and put your enemies to shame. He didn't send them to him either. Don't expect to prosper because of your honest life, your daily work and self-sacrifice. Don't think, because you go to church and pray, that he'll see that you have a long and comfortable life.

We confess Jesus Christ — the crucified.

3 WHO LABOUR AND ARE HEAVY LADEN. Somewhere in the depths of your soul you believed that your Sundays would always be sunny, your winters snowy, and that in your summers the blue sky would always smile. You would be able to develop your talents, without obstacles, for the good of others. And yet your years go by with you rushing around in labyrinths, wearing your-self out in the struggle for somewhere to live, for clothing, food and a job.

Somewhere in the depths of your soul you were sure. If you only showed people a bit of goodwill, a little good humour and friendliness, you'd win them over. But no, you have to go on beating your head against the stupidity around you, battle your way through malice and, with changing fortune, leap over traps people have set for you.

You haven't been spared anything. You have had to put up with everything a human being can put up with, and you can be sure that if there's something that hasn't hit you yet, it will. Somewhere in the depths of your soul you thought that only He had to have such a life, riven with the hypocrisy, the stupidity and the hatred of his enemies.

4 THE DISCIPLE IS NOT GREATER THAN HIS MASTER. It wasn't just his life that was like that. Every life is like that. Even yours. You too have periods of success, in which you are surrounded by the recognition and admiration of many friends. But periods of failure and defeat come, in which some friends betray you, others deny you — and you are left alone. People will pass unfair judgments on you, treat you like a fool. You carry your cross in the midst of incomprehension and contempt, hunted like an animal. You fall and get up, stung by cat-calls and jeers.

It wasn't just him who suffered like that under the cross. You do too.

5 EVERYONE WHO IS OF THE TRUTH LISTENS TO MY VOICE. Jesus died for the truth. Only a person who speaks as he thinks is his disciple, even when he doesn't do it in his name, yes even if he gives him no acknowledgment at all. The person who doesn't have the courage to speak the truth is not his disciple. Even if he thinks he is.

6 AND YOU WILL RISE AGAIN. Maybe you'll fall. Maybe you'll lose. Maybe you'll lose precisely because you try to live your life according to the model of Jesus. Your unselfishness is exploited

by others. Nobody notices your decency, nobody rewards your efforts; you don't hit the jackpot. You are labelled a dreamer, a naive, unrealistic, unpractical person.

You may fall. You may lose. But in the way that he lost, in the way that he fell.

7   HE CARRIED HIS CROSS. It's easiest to see the cross on Jesus' shoulders. It's a bit harder with our neighbour's cross. Most difficult of all is seeing our own cross. Seeing and believing could be our salvation.

8   HE WILL RISE AGAIN. Where are the palms in our hands? Where is the 'Hosanna' on our lips? But perhaps you're looking from a safe corner, full of anxiety, at Jesus' trimphal entry into Jerusalem. And perhaps you can already see the tragedy coming and damp the enthusiasm of the others.

Do you trust him? Do you believe he's right? Are you convinced that this way of his is right and honest, that the human race keeps returning to this way, that Jesus will always rise again? If you do, why are you hiding, why are you so put out, so suspicious, so unbelieving? Perhaps you just don't believe in him.

9   TO CARRY IT BEHIND JESUS. In the last resort you always come back to the way of the cross.

The deepest seclusion, the pleasantest pastime, even the greatest love, is not a protection against suffering. It can come at the moment of greatest happiness. Suddenly, like a tornado.

In the last resort you always come back to the way of the cross. But there you meet Jesus, going along with his cross.

10   I AM A KING. It was not Pilate who condemned Jesus, though all the appearances pointed to that. It was Pilate who was condemned. Even as he spoke the judgment. Jesus told him when he said, 'He that delivered me up to you has the greater sin'.

So Jesus was Pilate's king. Pilate stood before his king.

Don't make yourself ridiculous. Don't condemn the good Lord. Don't insist that he should explain himself to you, to say why he has given you such a life, why he has sent you suffering. Don't rebel. Don't threaten. He is your king. He has called you to life without asking your opinion; he guides you according to his will, even if it seems to be the other way round.

He will also recall you, whatever you feel about it.

Don't make yourself ridiculous. Don't insist that he should explain why he created the world as it is and not differently, or why there is so much suffering on this earth. He is king of the world. He made it, guides it according to his will, and calls people away from it when he wishes.

11 HAVE YOU COME OUT WITH SWORDS AND CLUBS TO CAPTURE ME? Do you acknowledge a king like this: with a crown, yes, but one of thorns, on a throne, yes, but that throne: the cross? A king who went to death for the truth and forgave his enemies as he died?

Do you acknowledge such a Jesus? Or perhaps you regard this situation as transitory and would rather wait for him to rise and start giving our bread. Perhaps you only acknowledge a Jesus who gives out bread.

12 HE HUNG BESIDE HIM. No one is accusing you or arguing with you. Jesus is just hanging on the cross, and everything is clear. Without any preaching. He just hangs there, and you don't dare to raise your eyes and look at him. You feel that you are cheap, false, you deceive others, you are comfortable, ordinary, very small.

13 LET HIM BE CRUCIFIED. Who shouted, 'Crucify him!'? Where was his friend Lazarus then? Where was the young man from Nain with his mother? Where were the lepers, paralytics and cripples he had cured? Where were the people he had fed with bread, the hundreds and thousands who had listened to him for three years, who had followed him, pushed round him and not

given him a pause for breath? Where were the people who only three days before, when he entered Jerusalem, had spread clothes under his feet and thrown palm branches over him,
Perhaps they too were now shouting 'Crucify him!'

14 AND IF HE SINS AGAINST YOU SEVEN TIMES IN THE DAY. We, the children of Cain. We cannot take a single step without treading on something. We cannot put a hand anywhere without crushing someone. We cannot give without taking. We cannot laugh without wounding the sorrowful. We cannot praise without injuring those we do not love.

And you'd like to stand there bright and clear, with clean hands, a glowing example. And the slightest criticism, the mildest accusation, sends you into a rage. And yet your hands are dirty.

15 IN THIS SINFUL GENERATION. Hate is slumbering within us. Of everyone, but especially of all those who are stronger, cleverer, faster, younger, more gifted, prettier, more powerful or richer. And particularly of those who are in competition with us and threaten us. Particularly of those who have made themselves unpopular with us, sometimes by a single word, a glance or an action. Even though we are restrained by forms of politeness, outward thoughtfulness, rules, social institutions we belong to, and social ties, we give vent to our feelings in an insult, a slander, through malice, contempt or disparagement.

Hate is slumbering within us. If you can grow out of it, it will be through God's grace and your heroic self-mastery.

16 WHOEVER SAYS TO HIS BROTHER, 'YOU FOOL!'. Do you know that you can get wild with rage, that your character collapses, your principles, ideals and good habits burst like a soap-bubble? You cease to be in control of your thoughts, words and movements. Swept away by a wave of madness, you start doing the stupidest things, hitting people and wounding them. Maybe you even destroy your life for good. And it's no good if you then start tearing your hair, beating your head against the

wall and saying, 'How could I do it?' It will then be too late for anything. You can no longer call anything back or change anything. Nothing will bring the original situation back.

Do you know you can get wild with rage? If you do, learn to listen to the murmuring of the avalanche swelling inside you so that you can stop it while there's still time. A moment later it will be too late to do anything. That remains true whether you're still a child, a young person or an old person.

17 OF LITTLE FAITH. A small-minded person is aggressive. He suspects everyone of wanting to destroy him. He is a mass of inner wounds and complexes. of presumption and prejudice. There is no way through to him. You can't even stroke him. Whatever you say to him, however you behave towards him, he sees everything as an attack on his identity. He has set himself only one goal, to preserve himself from destruction.

Do not be afraid. No one can destroy you provided you don't want to be destroyed.

18 IT WILL COME BACK TO YOU. Every evil that you do will in the last resort come back to you. The smallest mistake or inadequacy, the slightest dishonesty, the smallest injustice you do will relentlessly strike back at you, multiplied and in situations where you least expect it.

The only crumb of comfort is the fact that each of your good deeds will come back to you in the same way.

19 HE WENT ON. If only you knew. If you knew that you're getting further away. But you think you're going forwards.

If only you knew that you are wasteful, lie, deceive, waste time, are dishonest. But you think you live sensibly, rationally, modestly.

If only you knew that you're doing wrong. But you have a whole bundle of motives at your disposal, a precise system of justifications. You've built it up after your defeats, after painful experiences, after successes and victories. So pay attention to

uneasy stirrings of your conscience, to warning lights which come
on in you. It is your only chance of repentance.

20 HAVE YOU UNDERSTOOD ALL THIS? THEY SAID TO HIM,
    'YES'. You look at your neighbours, at their behaviour, listen to
    what they say — and you can't for the life of you imagine how
    they can still regard themselves as Christians. They ignore the
    essential truths, take only fragments of them and then interpret
    them in different ways. Have they any idea what Jesus is talking
    about?
       And people look at you and wonder how you can call yourself
    a Christian. People listen to you, look at your actions and doubt
    whether you understand anything about the Gospel.
       And yet we've been listening for so many years now to God's
    word, receiving it and feeding on it.

21 YOUR LIGHT. You look yourself in yourself and don't trust
    anyone any more. You try to organize your life all on your own
    and rely only on what you yourself can achieve, control and plan.
       You have no love any more. Claim there's no point in sacrific-
    ing yourself or fighting for justice for someone. You tremble for
    your health, fear for your money and your time. You forgive
    nothing, let nothing pass.
       People say of you that you've become a cynic, an egoist,
    you've changed. The light has gone out in you. You are empty.
    The arguments for and against God's existence don't concern you
    any more; they're unimportant to you because he isn't in you any
    more.
       People say you've changed, you used to be different. You
    yourself can remember those days, when you used to lead an
    open, broad life, when you sacrificed time, energy and money for
    others. Now you look back at those years almost with suspicion.
    Could you once live like that?
       Then there was light in you.

22 WHOEVER IS WITHOUT SIN AMONG YOU. We are all sinners, so why do you reach for the stone when you see sin in someone else? Why this zeal, this indignation, this self-righteous intolerance? After all, it has simply happened that his sin became known and yours remained hidden. And after all you don't know whether his sins are greater than yours, since you don't know how much he has received and how much you have. All of us are sinners. Each of us. So why do you want to throw the stone? Why don't you give the other person a chance? Why do you try to kill?

And perhaps you're even doing it in the name of truth or Christian love.

23 THEY ARE LYING IN WAIT FOR YOU TO KILL YOU. Don't pick up the stone they threw at you. Don't touch it. If you do, you'll be infected by hatred. Like lightening it will spread in you, take possession of you, eat you up like a cancerous growth. You'll soon be like your enemies. They are not killing you; you are destroying yourself.

Don't bend down for the stone they threw at you. Go on.

24 YOU CANNOT SERVE GOD AND MAMMON. Do not sell yourself for mammon. Do not sell your deepest experiences, your greatest mysteries and deepest convictions. Don't sell your friends — for the mammon of success, recognition, admiration, promotion.

At the end it will turn out that you have not won anything, but lost everything.

25 AS WE FORGIVE. How hardhearted we are towards our neighbours. We always want to put their head on the block. But you must accept other people as they are, with all their faults. Even when they turn out to be guilty of some dishonesty towards you. Forgiving is not forgetting. That is impossible. Forgiving is accepting someone with these sins they have committed against you. And then making up your mind to journey on in their company.

26 HE BEAT HIS BREAST. Examine yourself when you want to do something wrong, and you'll soon find arguments to justify your actions — for fear that you'd have to deprive yourself of something you're fond of, or for fear that someone might snatch away some advantage you've won, or through panic at consequences, such as loss of position, money or good name.

So be ruthless with yourself. Call a lie a lie, deceit deceit, theft theft, falsehood falsehood. Otherwise you'll become false, and there'll be no ground under your feet. Finally everything you want will be good, and everything you don't want will be bad.

27 AND THEY WILL NOT LEAVE ONE STONE UPON ANOTHER. The time of your great friendships is over. Friendships that grew out of enthusiasm for the world, for human beings, and for God. How many friends have you got left? How many have you sold out for money, for a higher status, for a better position? Or did you just give them up carelessly? Now too you have people you call friends, but the relations between you are structured by the principle of hard bargaining: I'll give you as much as you give me. Where is the time of your great friendships? How many have you got left?

Have you also lost your friendship with God?

28 I WILL BE CLEAN. Our lepers — the alcoholics, the wasted talents, the failed minds, the fallen angels, our former comrades. We look at them with disgust and contempt. We avoid them in order not to be infected by their misfortune. But they are our victims. With the help of our cronies we carefully edged them out of our circle. They didn't fit, they might have threatened our peace and security. They were robbed of their chance to be active in their field. They were not heard. They were cut off from all contacts.

You have your leper. You watched coldbloodedly as he took increasingly poor jobs and lost them one after the other. You watched him deteriorate, and now you shake your head over the fate of a man you brought into this state. You — an upright person, a responsible colleague, a respected citizen.

And it would have been enough for you to touch him. But maybe you still have a chance.

29 YOUR AUTHORITY. It's partly your fault that your superiors are as they are. It is partly your fault that they don't know the truth about themselves and their behaviour. You bow too low before them; you are too polite, you have said too many fair words to them on various festive occasions, too often you nod approvingly, express your respect and fawn.

So don't be surprised that they don't take you or others seriously if everything they hear only confirms their opinions, or that they regard it as a useful lesson to humiliate you and other subordinates. Don't be surprised that they don't discuss, but only make assertions, that they don't speak, but only make speeches, that they've got out of the habit of saying thank you or apologizing, that they don't live, but celebrate their lives, that they don't act normally.

But don't forget one thing. You are not the only one who has superiors; you are also in authority over others.

30 THE WATER THAT I SHALL GIVE WILL BECOME A SPRING OF WATER WELLING UP TO ETERNAL LIFE. How can we guard against losing the most precious gifts? It is so easy for us to turn a friend into a servant; if someone gives us his trust, we make him our slave, we make someone's love for us into a source of slavish adoration. We misuse a vocation — the divine spark — to create a comfortable, quiet little nook for ourselves. We reduce Christianity to an abstract system of truths.

How can we prevent the treasures given to us from declining into habits, empty words, hollow gestures?

31 LIKE YOURSELF. Be kind to yourself. Don't try to change everything in yourself straight away. Don't expect immediate results from your resolutions. Don't be upset by failures. Don't get hysterical when you've done something stupid, don't punish yourself too harshly, don't push yourself. Learn to wait out

periods when your head hurts, when you're sad, when you don't want to do any work, when you're sick of life. Make use of the times when you're in a good mood. Create incentives for your activity; promise yourself rewards. Be a patient educator of yourself, as you try to be of others.

April

Why are you so sad?

1 WHY ARE YOU SAD? This must be one of the most beautiful
sections of the Gospel. The wide band of the road, the cloudless
sky, the sun, and two slowly moving figures. And then the third
figure of the stranger. A scene which came to an end somewhere
at the entrance to an inn, as the sun went down and a coolness
fell over the earth.

We are like these disciples.

We followed Jesus of Nazareth when he was mighty in word
and deed before God and the whole people. But suddenly he
died. We went back to our houses, returned to tending our
gardens and looking to see if the fruit was ripening. But some of
our women frightened us. They had been at the tomb before
daybreak. They hadn't found his body, but had seen angels who
said, 'He is alive'. And some of our people went to the tomb and
found it as the women had said, but they did not find him.

So very frightened, anxious, unbelieving; so drained, so sad.

Unless we recognize him. In the breaking of the bread.

2 HE HAS RISEN. When you were a child, the sky at Easter was
always fantastically blue. And there was always a lot of sunshine
and green grass.

Even when it was cold, Mother would put on her thinnest
stockings. When Father had finished shaving, he would run his
hand over his cheeks, smile into the mirror and say, 'Ah, I'm not
that old yet', and put on his best tie. You would go to church in

your best suit. Your friends would have something new to wear, new shoes for the boys, a new spring coat for the girls. You would wait impatiently until the priest finally finished his sermon and then would go home to breakfast. The table would be covered with a white cloth, and there would be catkins in a vase.

Mother would put a big cake on the table. In front of you would be a cup of the best coffee, such as you never got anywhere except at your parents'. Memories like this of the feast of the Lord's resurrection have stayed with you from childhood.

And later, when you were a young man, when life took you out into the world and you believed in your strength and your successes — that was still too early to understand what resurrection is.

But imagine a time many years later. An Easter will come with a pale sun and a washed-out sky. In the mirror your wrinkled face with its grey stubble shocks you. You haven't gone out because you're not strong enough to any more. You stand at the window and watch as little streams of water run away between patches of dirty snow and the grass begins to turn green. The buds on the chestnuts are bursting. On the dry pavement slabs children are playing, just like you not so very long ago.

Maybe then you'll understand what resurrection is.

Part of the power of Christianity is that it guarantees life to you and anyone facing decay.

3 THEN THE OTHER DISCIPLE, WHO HAD REACHED THE TOMB FIRST, WENT IN, SAW AND BELIEVED. We came back with the apostles from the empty tomb. We, along with the three women, saw the angel who said, 'He is no longer here. He has risen'. He appeared to us in the garden, as we looked for him with Mary Magdalen. He told us that we shall see him again.

4 THE DOORS WERE SHUT, BUT JESUS CAME. He will come to everyone, as he came to them. To everyone, whether they are buried, unloved, forgotten or expected — whether they live in happiness or sorrow.

He will come to let you touch him, to let you believe that

your carrying of the cross, your wounds and your isolation are not in vain. To show you that all this is not in vain.

5   HE HAS RISEN FROM THE DEAD. How many times have they buried you already? How many times has the stone of calumny rolled over you? How many times have they confirmed your absence? And you have risen. Rumours go around that you've been seen in the street, you had a smile on your face — as in the past, in the finest days of your success and fame. People are beginning once more to talk about you with respect, to admire your cleverness and endurance, to understand your intentions correctly, to recognise your merits. And your enemies are beginning to get worried, those people who pronounced judgment on you, crucified you and buried you.

Don't think it'll be the last time. They'll bury you many a time yet. Many a time yet there will be rejoicing over your death. But you will rise. Without wanting to believe yourself that you're capable of it, you'll go around again and meet people being friendly to you again.

Truth always wins. Justice is everlasting. As long as you don't betray it, as long as you keep on serving it.

6   THAT YOUR JOY MAY BE FULL. It's getting on for evening. The day is more than half over. We're already twenty, thirty, sixty years old. We keep regretting that there are already so many years behind us and we are incapable of valuing the moment you give us.

Please teach us to enjoy life. No, not just not to get annoyed, but to enjoy ourselves. Always. Irrespective of how many years of experience already lie behind us, of how much trouble, worry and daily irritation we have to cope with.

Come to us as we go sadly through life, as you came to the disciples on the road to Emmaus. Bring us to our senses — like them. Open our eyes, before it's too late.

7   AND ARE YOU SAD? Even now we must live a bit of ascension. Even now we must go about the earth a bit, taking the risk of believing and trusting, against all the predictions. And loving and being happy all the more, even if sometimes we have little reason to.

Even now we must go about the earth a bit. That, against all appearances, is the only key to life. They will follow such people in long processions, coming like moths to the fire and bees to honey — all those calculating, just and yet so terribly sad people? To experience a little carefree belief, a little uncalculating hope, a little love that doesn't cost anything, a little happiness, without which it is impossible to live.

Even now we must live a bit of ascension.

8   I AM THE LIVING BREAD WHICH CAME DOWN FROM HEAVEN. That was the most important time for him, the time of suffering and death. In that time he defined himself, his relation to God, his Father, and to human beings.

The night before he instituted the eucharistic meal for us. By carrying out his testament we meet him in the holy mass, to take part in his suffering and death and from that to draw strength for everyday life: so that we may love people as he loved them and so that our death may end like his death, with resurrection in God.

9   LORD, GIVE US THIS BREAD. What we have left of that supper is the altar — a fragment of a table, the wafers and a little wine. That is his feast, to which he has invited us: his bread, his wine, his life. He wants us to share in this life.

What we have left of that supper is the altar — a fragment of a table, the wafers and a little wine. They are our gifts, which we have brought to him, for him to accept and look on as his own — so that our life may become like his.

10   IN THE TEMPLE. When we take part in the mass, how far removed are we from the faith of the apostles in the room of the Last Supper? How often we go to church on Sunday, driven by

tradition and habit. And then the question surfaces: should I, have I the right to go to mass like that, in that state? Is it really worth it?

Yes. Even if just every so often we bring home from mass some confidence, an idea, a conviction which keeps us from doing wrong, shows us the way, helps us to overcome our smallness — it is worth it.

11   THIS IS THE BREAD WHICH CAME DOWN FROM HEAVEN. Increasingly aware of our abandonment to death, so greedily grasping for life, we go every Sunday to the Lord's table. To the table of him who died, but rose again, who said he was the life, and that anyone who believed in him would live, even if they died.

12   THE TRUTH WILL MAKE YOU FREE. Take the other person seriously. Guard against sentimentality and against disparagement, against effusiveness and against irony, against easy excuses and against offhand criticism, against leniency and against indignation. Take the other person seriously even — or especially — when he or she seems to be provoking you to do precisely the opposite.

Only in that way can you help them to see themselves in the truth.

13   HE FORGAVE HIM THE DEBT. You can't base your dealings with other people solely on the principle of justice: you've given them so much and they owe you so much. You have to deduct so much as loss and forget so much, even if you get no thanks for it.

Don't think you're the only person who behaves like that. Look around. Other people near you are doing the same.

14   DO NOT JUDGE. You can have no idea why a person has acted in the way he has. Perhaps something has depressed him, perhaps he has had some sort of trouble. And even if he was in a normal state, you still don't know the motives by which he was

51

guided. You attribute to him one of those which — according to your logic — must have guided him. For that reason your judgment has little prospect of being right.

15 WHOEVER SAYS TO HIS BROTHER 'YOU FOOL' WILL BE LIABLE TO THE HELL OF FIRE. Fight with someone else when it is necessary, but don't kill him. Learn to discuss with him, contradict him, but don't treat him with contempt. Try never to give someone the impression that his remarks are unnecessary, because he doesn't know about anything and certainly has nothing important or interesting to say, in other words that he knows nothing and is nothing. First of all, it's not true. Second, if he believed it, you would drive him to despair.

Guard against believing that everything clever, important and interesting has been said by cleverer people than you, and all that's left for you to do is to chew over golden thoughts and truths already discovered. If you think like that, you kill everything creative in you. Your humanity is in danger.

16 HE BENT OVER HIM. Never give someone else the impression that you've stopped regarding him as the person he is making every effort to be. Your attitude could cause him to stop seeing the point of his efforts — and give up.

Never give someone else the impression that you regard him as a bad person. Even if he sees your opinion as wrong, it may undermine him and open barriers in him which he uses to protect himself from wrongdoing.

17 THROUGH WHOM THE OFFENCE COMES. Why are our children like this? Where do they get all this disregard for obligations, roughness, rudeness, indifference, contempt, selfishness, cunning, egoism and crudeness? Where do they get these expressions, this language, this tone? Why do they trample so brutally on the results of our work and so carelessly disturb our peace?

Don't say it's the parents. It's all of us! They are flesh of our flesh, blood of our blood. They are the children of our society.

We bear the responsibility for them.

18 SO THAT YOU MAY BE SONS OF YOUR FATHER. What is objectively true or who is right is not the only important thing. It is also important that someone else thinks something is true, is deeply convinced of something and wants to live accordingly. Everyone has an obvious right to do this, and you have an obligation to respect that right.

It is the basis of that form of justice which is called tolerance.

19 AND WHEN HE HAS FOUND IT, HE LAYS IT ON HIS SHOULDERS. You listen and can't believe your ears. You read and can't believe your eyes. The person who yesterday was proclaiming irresponsible, untenable ideas, is today beginning to speak and write normally. A fickle opportunist?

Perhaps he is one of those who were called in the last hour, perhaps one of those whom God touched and who became able to see, whom he touched and who suddenly began to hear. Perhaps he is one of the lost sheep that he found.

It is hoped that you are not one of the row of Pharisees and Sadducees who accuse Jesus because he eats with sinners and tax-collectors.

20 LET WHAT YOU SAY BE SIMPLY 'YES' OR 'NO'. What is this freedom of ours, this tolerance of ours? Perhaps it is simply fear of facing the truth squarely, fear of taking a mature decision with all the possible painful consequences, the attempt to put it off to the next day, and then to the next — as far away as possible.

What is this kindness of ours? Perhaps just laziness, which won't let us analyze or explore something to the bottom.

And so we live day by day with these people to whom we should have spoken the truth plainly, and didn't. We stumble over heaps of things that have remaind unfinished. We lead a life of pretence. The deposits of untruth, half-truth and lies grow. We become wormeaten, moulder away in these constant evasive manoeuvres, in these unsolved problems.

Until contempt for yourself grows and grows in you, disgust at people swells up in you to such an extent that you begin to find life revolting. And you recognize your own guilt.

21   WHAT YOU SAY. Talk to the person next to you. Silence only stays neutral for a short time. It quickly changes into distance, hostility, even hate. Only silence towards a friend cannot be a threat.

22   WOE TO THE WORLD FOR TEMPTATIONS TO SIN. We are unrivalled individualists. We take offence at the idea that others are our equals; we don't even want to think of the extent to which we are the product of preceding generations, we don't even want to know that our death won't mean that the whole world will collapse. We want to see our personal value saved at least in the context of our generation; we are not capable of saying 'brother' or 'sister' to another person.

However old you are, you go on. Believe it; you are only a leaf on the tree called humanity. Don't act as though you couldn't hear the steps of the next generation behind you — steps which are becoming more and more distinct. Realize that it is looking at you. It will be like you. You are responsible for this generation which is coming after you, and for all the subsequent ones.

23   IF YOU WILL. Don't force anyone to do anything, even if you are quite sure of yourself. Even in the case of something bad threatening someone, even in the case of a good thing bringing great benefits. Don't make anyone happy by force. Everyone has the right to be a human being, and free choice alone defines a human being. That alone makes a human being.

24   IF YOU HAD BEEN HERE, MY BROTHER WOULD NOT HAVE DIED. Until it happens. Then there is exasperation, heads are shaken, people savour every detail. And it turns out that it was in fact a long, gradually culminating process. For a long time

there had been talk about it over coffee, telephone conversations were suddenly broken off, people whispered to each other that his danger was growing.

But there was no one to help.

'I was hungry and you gave me no food, I was thirsty and you gave me no drink'.

25   I AM NOT WORTHY TO UNTIE THE THONG OF HIS SANDALS. 'Take these drops before you go to bed and this powder three times a day after meals; but the most important thing for you is rest. It would be best if you could get away somewhere, just cut yourself off from your previous surroundings and forget everything . . .!'

'I'll prescribe you another pack of these injections, and when they're over come back. But please remember, they only help if you don't get excited. You mustn't get upset, take a rosier view of the world . . .'

In many obituary notices and on gravestones instead of 'In unquenchable grief: Husband, children, grandchildren and daughter-in-law', instead of 'In respectful memory', instead of 'Our beloved mother', instead of 'from loyal colleagues', it should say, 'Your children worried you to death', 'The boss finished him', 'The rumours were the last straw'.

I don't know if he's a saint, but I do know he can shut a door quietly.

26   SHEEP AND WOLVES. The wicked Herod and the good shepherds exist only in nativity plays.

Listen to what married couples say when they split up. Listen to what the moter-in-law says about it, and what the daughter-in-law says. Listen to the comments pupils make about their teachers and teachers about their pupils. Listen to what children think of their parents and the other way round.

When one side spoke, there was no doubt in the matter at all for you. Everything was quite clear; the other side's guilt was plain to see. When you heard the other side, you didn't know any more.

If you had gone about it the other way and first heard the other side, it would have been the same.

The wicked Herod and the good shepherds exist only in nativity plays. When it's a matter of misunderstandings with other people, just don't put yourself in the ranks of the good shepherds or the three wise men.

27   AS WE FORGIVE. There is a saying, 'If you want to go into a house guarded by dogs, first throw a bone among them'.

The difference between people and dogs is that the dog can gnaw for, say, half an hour, but a person can spend his whole life at it. Sometimes it's about a critical remark, a rent increase, about who in the house is supposed to clean the stairs, sometimes it's about a rung in their professional career.

A ship which set out on a long journey was to meet different countries, people of different types and skin colour, was to go through sunrises and sunsets, days of calm and storm; but straightaway, on its maiden voyage, just outside the harbour, it ran on to a sandbank. And there it stayed. At an angle, overhanging the dirty water which washes over its sides, it looks at the old houses with the unlovely roofs and at the trees withering around them.

Learn to forgive. That means: forget.

28   AS WE ALSO HAVE FORGIVEN OUR DEBTORS. Buy a red dummy for the eternally bawling brat next door. Be the first to say 'Good morning' to the stuck-up hag across the road. Offer the landlord your hand, and ask him, without any innuendo, if he slept well. Tell the boss a joke. Put some flowers on the desk of the elderly lady in your office. Invite your mother-in-law to the cinema. Wash the son-in-law's socks. And one more thing. Give a smile to the nervous and jumpy assistant in the shop. The same with the shabbily dressed conductor in the tram. Give the policeman on the corner a smile, and the ugly child on its way to school. Smile to the old lady with the little dog.

And maybe God will give you the grace, and something like scales will fall from your eyes. You see around you the sad, the tormented, broken and depressed. Maybe you'll even understand more: that the cause of all this human distress is loneliness. And that only God can overcome this loneliness — and you, when you unite yourself to him and are kind.

29   NO ONE IS GOOD BUT GOD ALONE.
        Where does relaxation begin and idleness end?
        Where does firmness end and rigidity begin?
        Where does love of truth end and naivety begin?
        Where does criticism end and malice begin?
        Where does loyalty end and ingratiation begin?
        Where does rectitude end and brutality begin?
        Where does friendliness end and weakness begin?
        That is the split which is your daily bread.

30   I GIVE THEM ETERNAL LIFE. In the supernatural order too we construct a closed system. Someone must suffer for the madness of another; someone must pray so that a person gone astray may repent, through someone's renunciation the grace of repentance comes on the sinner. Our holiness influences the holiness of others; our sinfulness helps to determine whether and to what extent others become sinful. Only in this system does it become possible to see the point of strict monasteries, which give themselves over completely to prayer and self-renunciation. Only then does every good deed, even if nobody notices it, every good thought, every act of divine love, find its truly social meaning.

May

The mother of my Lord

1 HE SAID TO HER, 'WOMAN'. So angelic, so greatly blessed, that she was almost super-human, unreal.

And yet she was an ordinary woman. In the heat of Palestine's sun, in an ordinary dress, tied with a cord, a scarf on her head. She knew the way to the spring well. She had walked it hundreds of times with her clay pot.

She was completely and utterly a human being.

The small stones cut her bare feet. Her hands were roughened by grinding grain and digging in dried-out earth. She had come to know very well what disappointed hopes are, and the meaning of the words: 'My thoughts are not your thoughts and your ways are not my ways'.

When she had conceived Christ, when what all Jewish women dreamed of came true in her, she devoted herself with all her soul to him who had made his dwelling in her. She loved him with the freshness of her young girl's heart. She thought of him while digging, while washing the dishes, while washing clothes. She sang for him. She was happy because of him. She knew what his future was to be, knew what was in store for him.

And she imagined the role she would have in his life. When people turned away from him, she would be his refuge, rest on his far-flung wanderings — the person who understood him best.

The reality was to turn out differently.

The first sign of this was when Jesus disappeared. She was in no way responsible. Clearly and openly she said to him, 'Son, why have you treated us so?' Behold, your father and I have been looking for you anxiously'. She received an answer which must have surprised her greatly.

'Did you not know that I must be in my Father's house?' She had not expected an answer like that. The evangelist was to write later, 'And they did not understand the saying which he spoke to them'. They saw a wall erected between their son and them. He had another world, to which they had no access.

Thirty years. Jesus left home to teach.

He went off and never came back. In the gospels there is no mention of Jesus coming back to visit his parents' home during his thirty years' teaching and preaching.

But his holy mother waited. Might he come? He had to come. After all, he knew she was waiting. And if he didn't come, why didn't he?

Months passed. Clouds of the hatred with which the Pharisees pursued Jesus piled up over him. Bad news came thick and fast. More or less sympathetic people brought it to her. They told her also about the slanders the Pharisees were spreading about Jesus. His enemies were looking for a pretext to condemn him to death, or at least to imprison him. The whole of Palestine knew their trick questions and the crushing replies Jesus gave.

But how she wished that he would come, have a rest, tell her about his life, or at least come, even without saying a word, come and sit down.

But Jesus didn't come. So she went to find him.

He was in some house disputing with Pharisees. They came and told him that his mother would wait outside, but Jesus did not go out.

And then perhaps something dawned on her. She realized that her road was a different one. He didn't want her to be a support or refreshment in his suffering. He wanted to suffer alone, alone to drink the bitter cup to the dregs. She could only watch from a distance and feel for him. God had marked out a different road for her, not the one she had imagined in her youth. She understood and accepted this road, even though it would cost her much self-denial. In the presence of Annas, Caiphas and Pilate, we no longer see her beside Jesus. Their eyes met once on the road to Calvary. At the end she stood under the cross, and even there she heard the word which was the last word she wanted to hear from his lips: 'Woman'.

2   HER SON. 'They're back'. She shuddered. They were already
pressing at the main gate, a chattering mob. She went stiff inside
as, after sarcastic greetings to the 'mother of the great master of
Nazareth', they started asking questions about his life. What had
he done? And — this was the main thing — what had he said? She
was appalled at these people's hatred. She knew that she ought to
say as little as possible, best of all say nothing. With unmerciful
eyes they looked at the place where he had worked, went through
his things, exchanged ambivalent remarks. And they quoted
phrases from his teaching. They seethed with malice. They shook
their fists in her face. Fancy bringing him up like that. What a
mother. Finally they advised her to use her influence on him,
since he didn't realize the danger he was in. It was a pity; he had
talent. They had him in their power, but out of sympathy for her
they didn't want to destroy him. Then they went. They left behind a deep silence, a dull pain in her breast, and the certainty
that they would come back, that they would leave her no peace.
Then they were back to get him. Their knocking at the door
roused her abruptly from a deep sleep. The red glare of the
torches burned her eyes. They rushed into the room. One stayed
with her, the others stormed through the house, and when, as
usual, they didn't find him, asked her where he was. They refused
to believe that he was really not there, hadn't been for a long
while. Or that she really didn't know where he might be. As they
left they swore at her. Perhaps God did not allow that one of
them should actually hit her.

When she went through the streets of Nazareth — the Nazareth
that after an address by Jesus in the synagogue wanted to kill him
— she could not escape whispers, remarks and shouts. Insistent
stares tried to force her to raise her eyes, tried to see her fear,
grief or anger. She felt alone, surrounded by contempt. She
followed him to Jerusalem. She was near him when he died. Then
she was alone again. And again there were the same whispers and
the same stares: 'That's the mother of that criminal they crucified
on Golgotha', 'The son of this carpenter from Nazareth who
incited the Jewish people'.

The joy of the resurrection was overshadowed by the spying and probing of the others. 'Why don't you go to your son's grave? He's not there? He's risen from the dead? Oh yes, where have you hidden him?'

Perhaps God did not allow that one of those who mocked her should actually spit at her. After that almost all the apostles scattered. Peter and John were persecuted, were summoned before the Sanhedrin, were constantly in danger and almost never showed themselves in public. Only sometimes, when it was dark and you could hurry through the streets without being seen, some of those who had loved him came to her and asked, 'Tell us about him'.

How do we know all this? Where did we hear it all, these footsteps outside the house, this knocking at the door, these questions about a son, this shouting, beating and torment? Why is she so close to us now? Because she went through what our mothers had to go through.

3   HIS MOTHER. She went along, the blue sky above her, the green hills all round and under her feet the dust of the road. For the first time in public, in front of all the people. Happiness and the delight that only mothers know.

Soon Simeon will foretell her sufferings. That will be her first sorrow, the first sword to fall on her on her son's account. Others follow. The twelve-year old's incomprehensible reply: 'How is it that you sought me? Did you not know that I must be in my Father's house?' Words which silenced the trembling question, born of anxiety and reproach, 'Son, why have you treated us so?' And later the strange words, so hard to accept, spoken at Cana in Galilee: 'Woman, my hour has not yet come'. The last time she heard that 'Woman' was under the cross.

But he is her son. In spite of everything, even if something a hundred times more painful had happened, if he had gone even further away — he is her son. She is his mother.

4   AND TOOK HIM UP IN HIS ARMS. When the wolves came right up to the farms, when a storm raged over the houses, our fore-

fathers would commend themselves to the protection of the mother of God and light candles.

Wolves don't threaten us any more.

It's not wolves that threaten us now.

Lightning doesn't threaten us any more.

It's not lightning that threatens us now.

At Mary's Candlemass we ask her to take us into her prototection. Protection against men who are wickeder than wolves, against misfortune which comes more suddenly than lightning.

5 HE TOOK HIM UP IN HIS ARMS. So many paths, roads, directions, signs, slogans, banners, lights, so much noise, so many attempts to persuade, appeals, orders, requests. So many stars.

But you — pushed by people rushing here and there in panic — hold Jesus tightly to you, to your heart, as his mother did as she went with him through the Temple.

Don't let yourself be frightened, shouted down, diverted, don't let yourself be led astray. Don't let him be knocked out of your hands. Then you'll reach your goal.

6 BY THE CROSS OF JESUS STOOD HIS MOTHER. The mother of Jesus. What sort of mother was she? She knew, of course, as well as anyone else in Palestine, the danger he was in. Everyone knew about his verbal battles with the Pharisees and Sadducees. She knew — the rumour went from mouth to mouth — that they sought his life, that they were looking for evidence 'to put him to death'. She knew, at least, that victory was out of the question, and that a path like his could only end in death. So why didn't she go and plead with him to leave his enemies alone? Why didn't she tell him not to attack them, not to confront them with their crimes, and, when they said things to him, to say nothing or answer evasively'. Why didn't she tell him to talk about love, but so generally that they weren't provoked? He could carry on going through the fields, could go on fishing expeditions at night with his disciples, in the noonday heat he could sit by Jacob's well and drink cool water, he could visit Maria, Martha and Mary in Bethany and enjoy their happiness.

What sort of a mother was she? Why didn't she come when he was brought before the court? Why didn't she come and promise the assembled Sanhedrin that he would go back to Nazareth, stop teaching and spend the rest of his life working as a carpenter? He could carry on brushing the hair out of his eyes with his work-worn hands, eating his bread in the quiet of his house and chatting to his friends as dusk fell.

What sort of a mother was she? Why didn't she come to Pilate as he pronounced sentence of death on her son, why didn't she come and beg for clemency. Let him be condemned to life imprisonment − in the galleys or the quarries, even the hardest and most degrading sort. He would at least be alive.

But she went silently with him as he carried the cross, stood there passive as he died.

That is why she is not just the mother of Jesus but also the mother of the saviour, the redeemer, our mother.

7 HE SAID TO THE DISCIPLE, 'THIS IS YOUR MOTHER'. If it bothers you, don't call her 'Queen'. If it sounds funny to you, don't call her 'Virgin'. If it has no meaning for you, don't call her 'Lady'. If you can't understand it, don't call her 'Vessel of the holy Spirit'. Just say 'you' or 'Mary'. Whatever you like, provided she is to you what she has to be − Mother.

8 BLESSED IS THE FRUIT OF YOUR WOMB. In her we honour those women who sacrifice a part of their lives for other people: watching through nights, seeing to the meals every day, washing nappies, worrying at every cough and temperature, days full of rushing about to get the work done. Later worrying about each independent step of the young person moving clumsily into life − all the time their own loneliness before their eyes.

In her we honour the women who have given the word 'love' its full content.

9 THIS IS YOUR SON. Who still wants to be a mother today, to be a person whose job it is to sacrifice herself?

Stay single! For ever, until death. Even if there are children. The nursery, the school, mother-in-law, friends, aunts, toys can educate them. The main thing is that they're not in the way, don't disturb you, don't hamper you, don't become a burden. The main thing is that they should be as little as possible at home. And so this word 'Mother' has disappeared. It has paled. We have lost it, we who look so hysterically for love.

10   MARY, HIS MOTHER. What do you think when you look at her as she prays at her annunciation, as she holds the child in her arms, as she stands on Golgotha, as she embraces his body when it has been taken from the cross?

What do you ask her for, what do you bring her, what do you hope for from her, what are you waiting for?

You — at the age of eighteen, thirty, seventy.

How do you pray to her?

11   THEY FOUND MARY. Believing in God means also believing in human beings. Trusting God means also trusting human beings. Loving God means also loving human beings.

If that is true, how can anyone not believe *her*, not trust *her*, not love a human being like *her*?

12   THE CARPENTER OF NAZARETH. When you were small, you wanted to be famous. You didn't know yet why, but you believed that the newspapers would carry reports about you in huge letters. Are you still waiting? Yes, we want people to notice us, ask us for things, thank us, to recognise and respect us. In the Gospel there are many figures which are very clearly drawn. About St Joseph we know little. Many sayings have been handed down, not only of the apostles but also of pharisees, tax-collectors and sinners. Of Joseph's not a single one.

We don't even know when he died. No one paid much attention to him.

He wanted to leave Mary when he found out that she was pregnant. He stayed when the angel told him to. When the angel told him to, he fled with Mary and the child to Egypt. When the angel told him to he returned to Palestine.

He submitted and obeyed, even if he didn't always understand the purpose of these instructions. He worked to keep the mother and son.

A patron of those who are not in leading positions, who stay hidden, whom we notice as little as the wind and yet need.

13 THE MOTHER OF MY LORD. Be a mother to us. Make us your children.

Make us able to come to terms with out fate as you did at the moment of the annunciation, to bear hardship like you when you gave birth to your child in the stable, to accept humiliations like you when you had to flee to Egypt, to look for Jesus as you did in the Temple in Jerusalem, to ask him for things as you did in Cana when the wine at the marriage feast ran out, to suffer like you when you stood under your dying son's cross, to pray like you in the room of the Last Supper when you waited for the coming of the Holy Spirit.

We ask you, make us your children. Be a mother to us.

14 FOXES HAVE HOLES. Human beings need homes. Not 'especially in these days', not 'more than ever'. Always. As long as human beings have been human and as long as they want to go on being human. Not four walls, not a hotel, not overnight lodgings, not a billet, but a source of peace, of refreshment, strength, love — a home.

15 THE FIRST AND GREATEST COMMANDMENT. To believe in God, to believe in people.

To believe that he will come, that he will not leave you alone, not betray you, not sell you out.

Believe in people. And even if they did betray you, even if they did go away, even if they did deceive you, you must carry on believing in the good that remains in them, that they are, that makes them what they are. Believe in people.

If you stopped believing in people, if you removed from your life all the people around you, faith in God would be impossible. Losing faith in people means losing faith in God.

16 BIRDS HAVE NESTS. You have to find your town on the map of the world, look for your way in the maze of streets, pick out familiar faces in the crowd, recognize friends' voices in the din, somewhere build your house.

You must have your own favourite author, your favourtie painter, reporter, announcer and commentator. You must have your books and newspapers, your theatres, your pictures in the galleries, your cinemas, cafés and restaurants. So that the world does not confront you cold and hostile, but is a home for you.

17 AND GOING INTO THE HOUSE THEY SAW THE CHILD WITH MARY HIS MOTHER. Do not enclose love within the four walls of your house. Don't think that love of your neighbour is exhausted in love for your family. It is easily transformed into cheap selfishness. A home should not be a castle, but a base. Your family affairs should not claim all your attention and energy — but help you to go out to those around you.

18 THOU SHALT LOVE THE LORD THY GOD. Marriage is not going through a crisis; we have a crisis in our faith in God, a crisis in our love for him. If you haven't enough faith, if you don't love him enough, you can search a hundred years for your ideal, you can find your girl or your man, you may have a wonderful time together — but it will come to an end. Human beings are finite creatures. Their skill and strength come to an end, and so do their kindness and attractiveness. Every human being longs for complete beauty and complete truth. That is why there are so many cases of love ending in sadness — human beings ask other human beings for what they cannot give.

19 DO NOT JUDGE. We are Christians only as long as we respect the mystery of the person next to us, as long as we bear in mind that none of our formulations or definitions is capable of doing justice to them. No sin extinguishes that mystery, no decision — positive or negative — ultimately determines their fate. We are Christians only as long as we are able to believe in others, to trust them and to love them.

20 INTO HIS HOUSE. We are becoming brutes. There is ever more brutality inside us. We injure each other. We wrong each other. In the street, on the bus, at work, at school. It gets worse and worse.

The fires in our hearths are growing cold. There is less and less of the maternal in our mothers, less and less of the paternal in our fathers. There are fewer and fewer real homes. Our houses are less and less places to live in. They are only hotels, lodgings for the night. The common table is disappearing. We fill our stomachs in odd corners, directly at the cooker, in front of a hotplate. Just so that we can get into the town as quickly as possible, well away from home where it is so boring and desolate.

We shan't build a world like that, no matter how advanced our technology. We are ceasing to be human.

21 THEY FOUND MARY AND JOSEPH AND THE CHILD. Since the start of its existence the human race has gone through so much, committed so many stupidities and enormous mistakes, so often burnt its fingers, but in moments of reason it always returns invariably to what is most important: the man, the woman and the child. More and more we come to realize, whatever further discoveries the human race makes, whatever revolutions it goes through, whatever achievements it produces, its basis, as long as it exists, will always be the man, the woman and the child. And the more experience we obtain, the more strongly we are convinced that there is no price the human race should not pay, no effort it should not undertake, to create the best possible conditions for this grouping, father, mother and child.

22 NEITHER BE CALLED MASTERS. From idleness we adopt the attitude of the master, the instructor — since it enables us to perform our educational task with the least expenditure of energy. Or from fear, because we are afraid that our empty, barren inner selves will be revealed. That is why you give sermons, moralize, admonish, threaten and give orders. That sort of training is mechanical, and any human being with any self-respect at all will reject it.

If you are really concerned about educating the people who are with you, if you really love them, come down from the lofty throne of the master and teacher. Love does not mean alms that the haves give to the have-nots, the rich to the poor, the powerful to the helpless, the strong to the weak. Anyone who has the slightest sense of dignity will reject that. Love means sharing. If you want to help someone, live with them. Then you give yourself to them at every moment. Even if you stand with a crown of thorns — spat at, laughed at, treated with contempt — you will do more teaching than if you had spent your whole life preaching — you will teach in that instant.

23 FOR THE SALVATION OF THE WORLD. What heights do you reach for? What do the words 'family', 'home town', 'nation', 'mankind' mean to you? What reaction do you have to patriotism? Do you get out of it by saying it isn't relevant to today? And your town? Do you smile indulgently at it? And where you work? Have you even a dismissive wave of the hand for it? How big are you? What grips you, grieves you or disturbs you? What things, what people? Your mother, your sister, your friend, your acquaintance, your colleague, a passer-by, a fellow countryman, some other person? Who do you worry about? Who is important to you? Who do you feel responsible for? What heights do you reach for? What are your horizons?

24 LOOK AFTER HIM. What is important is that your neighbour should experience kindness through you, that he should find himself in you, that, when he is broken, he should stand straight again, when he is extinguished, he should burst out in new fire, when he is crumpled he should bloom again. That in your company he should become a human being in the full sense of the word.

25 RAVENING WOLVES. It is not just others who take advantage of you, take up your time, make exorbitant claims on you, don't keep their commitments. You take advantage as well: when you are really in a desperate situation and ask for help, when you rely on others out of laziness, throw off your responsibilities on to them, make use of their time without scruple, forget to say please and thank you.

And it is far from certain whose account is more in the red, who takes more advantage.

26 WHO SEES IN SECRET. Watch yourself when people start showing appreciation, rewarding, singling out your close friends or professional colleagues and passing you over — even though everything may have started with you, or at least you put in hard work at it, although you know most about it, although it's mainly thanks to you that anything came of it at all.

Watch yourself most of all when you remain in the shadows and others are in the limelight. Put to yourself the question, 'Why did I do it all?' Really so that they'd talk about you, notice your contribution, recognise your work and admit that it was your initiative, your idea? Is that really the only reason why you took all the trouble?

27 SHEEP OF THIS FLOCK. The Church is not a collection of individuals each of whom, apart from the others, is simply concerned about the salvation of his or her own soul.

You are therefore a member of the Church, not just through baptism, but also because you feel a part of this group, can pray with them, are well disposed towards your brothers and sisters — because you help them to live.

28 AND HIS SWEAT BECAME LIKE DROPS OF BLOOD. It is easy
to believe among friends, when the sun shines above our heads —
in a time of peace.

But how are you to believe when enemies press you hard,
when they begin coldbloodedly to destroy you; when they take
from you what is a piece of yourself, drive you from your work,
which is part of your identity, when the block off the future on
which you are so set. How can you avoid panic, how can you not
be overwhelmed with despair, how can you avoid taking over
your enemies' methods, being infected by their hate. How is one
to believe when the times are inhuman?

29 PERFECT. You may not meet any criticism, but that doesn't
show that you are perfect and infallible. It may only show that
people haven't the courage to express criticism in your presence
because they have been led to believe that you won't accept it.
They have found that you regard yourself as perfect and infallible.

If no one ever admonishes you it means that things are very
bad in your neighbourhood.

30 ON FINDING A PEARL. What is your position among all those
who deny their human dignity, abandon their own opinions,
accept constant obedience and acquiescence, self-abasement and
self-contempt to make a career and a fortune for themselves?
How do you stand among those who pile up money with both
hands, drive others from their jobs, make their way upwards by
trampling others. How do you stand among those who are only
out to make new contacts, to acquire connections and support?
Are you at peace? Do you look at them with astonishment, with
horror, with pity, as you would at people who were sick, possessed, mentally ill or abnormal? Are you glad you're apart from
all that? Are you glad you have the gift of faith? Doesn't it hurt
you when they go on upwards, that they get rich, while you are
left behind? Is there not a grain of bitterness in you? Watch that
it doesn't grow into a tree.

31 AND FROM THAT HOUR THE DISCIPLE TOOK HER TO HIS OWN HOME. Be near us at the hour of our death.

Be near us at the hour of our suffering when those who we thought were friends injure us.

Be near us at the hour of our misfortune, when we injure someone — so that we recognise our guilt and try to make up for the evil.

Be near us now and at the hour of our death.

Faith is living in the light

1 WHOEVER DOES THE WILL OF MY FATHER. You say you believe because you acknowledge God's existence. But that is only the level of information, the level on which you take cognisance of something. That is still not faith. Faith in God means trusting in God and risking a life in brightness, honesty, truth and selflessness. Risking! The first step is directed against your own ego, your own egoism. But that is only the first step. Afterwards you believe because you are convinced that it's the only way to live. You become convinced by the happiness, the satisfaction, the inner light you bear within you.

Faith is living in the light.

2 RECEIVE YOUR SIGHT. Faith means recognizing the existence of a supernatural world, the existence of all of reality. To faith visible reality reveals itself as a section of a larger whole. Only with faith do all the aspects of visible reality find their definitive justification and explanation. Only with faith do we find an answer to the question of the meaning of the world, of the human race, each and every person, the questions of death and suffering. Only with faith can we fully and completely grasp the danger of evil and the greatness of good.

3 IF YOU HAD FAITH AS A GRAIN OF MUSTARD SEED. Have you ever travelled across the sea? Have you ever moved moun-

tains? Have you at least once in your life believed in what you were doing — in great things that you saw? Was your faith at least at one time really great, solid, steadfast? Do you carry on believing even when people try to persuade you that you shouldn't be so persistent, so demanding? And yet only when you believe can you experience a miracle, only then do the mountains of difficulties disappear, only then can you stride across abysses which open up under you, go over traps people set for you.

But perhaps you'd rather not believe? It's more comfortable, less dangerous, more peaceful not to trust oneself or other people or God. But then don't complain that you can't move mountains. Don't be surprised that the sea doesn't part before you. Don't be surprised that you're so tepid, so colourless, a nobody.

4 BE LIKE YOUR FATHER. What sort of a God do you believe in? In the one who's just, who rewards goodness and punishes evil. Strict too. Never overlooks any guilt, never forgets anything, never gives anything away. This God pursues you till you've paid everything back, to the last penny. Till you've paid for your wickedness, your mistake, your weakness, your stupidity. You feel his lash on your shoulder. Do you believe in a God like that?

Christ's God is a God who catches sight of the prodigal son from afar and runs to meet him. When the son falls at his feet, he lifts him up and brings him into his house. Christ's God is a God who, when one sheep is lost, leaves ninety-nine and goes out to look for it until he finds it.

Are you a Christian? Perhaps you are a just person, who gives nothing away, never forgets anything, never forgives anything, but is always pursuing until he's paid back to the last penny. Until every debtor has paid for his wickedness, for his mistake, for his stupidity.

5 TRUE GOD. Beware of carving a God for yourself in your own image and likeness and putting him away in a corner of your soul.

Beware of carving yourself a God in you own image and likeness and putting him away in a corner of your soul so that you can worship him there from time to time, say a prayer, and be glad that you have him and are a believer.

Believing in God is something different.

If you want to find out whether you believe, look at your life.

6   NO ONE HAS EVER SEEN THE FATHER. Though he is so simple that even a child can receive him, he is at the same time so complicated that even the greatest minds are at a loss before him.

Though he is so near that you can be united with him in prayer at any time, he is at the same time as distant as if worlds divided us from him.

Though he is so compassionate that even the worst sinner can obtain forgiveness from him, he is at the same time so just that even the greatest sinner cannot be sure of being saved.

Though he was born, lived and died like a man, he will always remain a mystery for us; he will always be beyond our senses, beyond our reach, beyond our thoughts — for the gulf of infinity divides us from him.

7   LORD, TEACH US. He has revealed himself to us, but that doesn't mean that he has told us everything about himself and that all that's needed to know him is to investigate further or ask the theologians.

He was born and died on the cross for us, but that doesn't give us the right to go around claiming the boldest intimacy with him.

He instituted the Church and the sacraments, but we should not let ourselves think that we have total control over the grace hidden in these symbols.

For us he remains a mystery, and that is the surest thing we know about him.

8   HELP MY UNBELIEF. Do not be misled by the example of official Christians who make piles of money in the service of God, make use of their power, consolidate their positions and every Sunday go to church and to communion. Are you sure that they believe?

Do not be misled by those who claim to believe neither in God nor in the help of our Lady, who do not go to church or to the sacraments and yet strive to live honestly. Do not be misled. Are you sure that they don't believe?

9 WHICH GOD HAS MADE. In one of the many milky ways which run through the universe there is a sun, which is like millions of other suns. Around it revolve planets of different sizes. On one of these planets lives man, whose existence, in comparison with the age of the universe, is not much longer than the time a match burns. He stands there, puts his hands in his pockets, and asks, 'Where is the creator?' In the end he is prepared to put the so-called God on a very fragile throne, but that comes later. For the moment God is suspected of not existing. Suspect on many other counts too. How could he become man and be born in a stable? How could he rise from the dead? How could he be one and at the same time three persons?

This approach won't get us anywhere. We must start from the position of the creature, not from that of the judge. From a position which every human being feels, whether he is simple or educated, the feeling of his own incompleteness, of his own unnecessariness. Only this position is honest.

10 COME TO ME. How difficult it must be for blacks to believe in Christ in view of the Christians who attacked their coastal villages, stole their ancestors and brought them in appalling conditions to America, where they were forced into super-human exertions. In view of the Christians who exploited their ignorance for so many centuries.

How difficult it must be for the Indians to come to believe in Christ in view of the Christians who murdered their people or demoralized them with alcohol, who brought them tuberculosis and took away their land.

How difficult it was for the Greeks and Romans to come to believe in Christ in view of the crude stories of primitive Jews who claimed to be witnesses to the redeemer.

How difficult it is for us to come to believe in Christ in the face of false, hypocritical Christians, in the face of the plain evil and stupidity of those who call themselves his followers.

How much longing for truth is needed here, how much good will — how much grace.

11   FIVE BARLEY LOAVES. It might have been like this. 'Please sit down.' Five thousand men sit down. 'I am the Son of God. That may seem unlikely to you, and so to confirm my words I shall work a miracle. Look on your right knees. Is there bread there?' And five thousand men reply, 'No, there is no bread on my right knee'. 'And now look at your left knees. Are there fish on them?' And five thousand men reply, 'There are no fish on my left knee'. And now everyone watches. A moment's silence, hands raised, an ecstatic look into the sky. Hey . . .! On every man's right knee is a loaf, and on his left are fishes.

But it was quite different. Jesus took a couple of loaves, broke them, blessed them, put them in baskets, added a couple of fishes, and told the apostles to distribute them. It's quite a business distributing something to a few thousand people. What experience of this event did each member of the crowd have? He saw quite simply that a disciple of the master of Nazareth gave him a loaf and a fish out of a basket.

12   AND THEY ALL FORSOOK HIM AND FLED. We believed in him because he preached the kingdom of truth, and we followed him enthusiastically because we believed in his victory. But a long time has passed since those days. The triumphal progress has somewhere been scattered to the four winds. We look round for our comrades and find with amazement that they have taken comfortable posts in the earthly kingdom while we are still living like the grass of the field and the birds of the air. And we feel cheated. But what did you expect? What were you looking for?

13   PRAY. With empty, upraised eyes, our stiff arms stretched out in front of us, we move forwards with unsteady steps. We collide with other blind people like ourselves, bump into objects, walls,

wander around in the labyrinth of alleys, misled by false voices, stumbling over stones, wading through puddles — trembling, uncertain, sad.

Don't you feel that there's another world? Doesn't the rustling of the wood reach your ears? Hasn't the warmth of the sun stroked your face? Kneel down on the road — Jesus is passing by — and call, 'Jesus, son of David, have mercy on me!' He will listen, but carry on calling, 'Jesus, son of David, have mercy on me!' Maybe people will tell you to be quiet, that there's no point. But don't stop, just ask. Quite certainly he will come to you and ask you, 'What do you want me to do for you?' 'Master, let me receive my sight again.' Quite certainly he will answer, 'Be it done to you as you wished.' And you will see, first Jesus and then this other world — full of colour, spacious, true.

14 YOUR KINGDOM. Finding the meaning of life. Knowing the point of being honest, the point of working, of bringing up children — the point of being alive.

Jesus said the kingdom of heaven was like a precious pearl, and when someone finds it he sells all he has to get it. He said it was like a treasure hidden in the field; when someone found it he sold all his possessions to acquire the field.

The kingdom of heaven opened for Zacchaeus when he recognized his faults; it will open for you too when you recognize the wrongs you have done.

The kingdom of heaven opened for the woman who was a public sinner when she fell at Jesus' feet and wept, but it opens for you too when you see your sins.

If only the sun doesn't dry up this grace and weeds don't choke it; if only the birds don't eat it up. If only you don't look for the excuse that there's no point to behave like that because people are hyenas and you have to be like them in order to live among them.

No, it's not true. A girl jumped from a second floor in order to remain pure. A railwayman threw himself in front of an oncoming train to pull a child off the line. A competitor on the world championship slalom admitted that he had missed out a gate which the judges hadn't noticed. These are not made-up stories, but things I found in the newspapers.

Take the individual little stones of grace, the red ones of love, the green ones of hope, the gold ones of smiles, all of which God gives you, and put them together to make your mosaic of the kingdom of heaven. Let it grow in you as the mustard seed grows into a great tree.

15 MY YOKE IS LIGHT. Don't you have the slightest regret, even for a moment, that you believe — that God has given you the gift of faith?

Is there no resentment in you that because of this faith you have to make decisions against your will, against your nature, decisions which are neither solidly based nor tested? That because of your faith you have a sad and difficult life, while you might live happily and in freedom?

If you think like that you have no conception of Christianity.

Christianity, Christ, asks nothing more of you than to be really a human being. If that involves pain, it is only because it is so difficult to be a human being. In reality, though, you long for nothing other than to be just that. Nothing else will give you more happiness.

16 NEITHER DO I CONDEMN YOU. Take care, or you will just wallow in human filth, pursue human passions, crimes and bad habits, analyze other people's failures, gaze in fascination at human vulgarity and depravity — to make it easier to bear the bitterness of your own failed life.

Life ought to be beautiful, with beautiful mornings and beautiful evenings, beautiful springs and summers. Life can still be beautiful.

17 WHO SEES IN SECRET. We fear the good Lord. We cannot bear his reality. We would rather put him in a world of unreality. We are ready to support objections to religion picked up anywhere, just for the sake of suppressing the reality of God's presence.

We fear loneliness, lest he appear to us face to face. We fear silence, lest he speak to us.

We barricade ourselves against him by constantly insisting on protestations of love and loyalty.

We don't want to need him. We elevate ourselves through positions, titles and other people's respect. We flee from him in duties, in pleasures and relaxation.

We drown him out with conversations, with music, song and noise.

We look for pardon in the unintelligibility of church rituals. We excuse ourselves with the boredom of sermons, with the dubious attractiveness of dogmas, with bad people who regard themselves as Catholics.

But in the depths of our souls we know that all this is no use, that he is there even if we don't want anything to do with him, that he speaks, even if we don't want to listen to him, that we meet him, however far we go to avoid him; that our meeting with him will be all the harder on the last day.

18 THE FATHER HAS LIFE IN HIMSELF. We fear the living God. That is why we give him a place somewhere in a distant heaven as the one who created the world, who made the laws of nature, who gave human beings once and for all the laws on the tablets of stone and now rests in total immobilitiy. And yet he is LIFE, ACTION, ACTIVITY. You can meet him on the difficult roads of your everyday life, only touch him with your work-worn hands, hear him, if you are capable of hearing.

It is easier to put God in a corner like an ideol to whom you from time to time throw a handful of incense and before whom you bow. But the truth is that because he is life, you can only meet him through your life.

19 HE WEPT BITTERLY. Was Jesus wrong when he called Peter a rock against which the gates of hell would not prevail? In the end Peter denied him before the first cock crew. Wasn't Jesus wrong to found his Church on such a rock?

Doesn't the Church exaggerate when she calls Paul the apostle of the gentiles, Paul who had such an ominous past?

Peter and Paul are symbols of the Church, because people of that sort are always important in the Church, people who have left everything and followed Jesus, even though they may have had dubious pasts. In the Church the great gesture which wipes out even the worst sins is always valid. In the Church what Jesus said to the sinful woman always applies — she was forgiven much because she had loved much.

20   I BELIEVE THAT YOU ARE CHRIST. Do you believe in Jesus? Does he appear in the motives of your actions. Do you at least sometimes decide one way and not another because you think he would have decided that way? Is he a model for you?

Or perhaps you just believe in God, not in Jesus?

21   PRAY THEN LIKE THIS: OUR FATHER. We are proud. How could it be otherwise when we have as master him who drove the dealers out of the Temple with strokes of a whip, who said to the Pharisees and Sadducees — the leaders of his nation — 'Woe to you, brood of vipers; you are like white-washed tombs'. We are proud. We don't put our heads in the dust, don't bow our foreheads to the ground before God — the Lord, the Ruler, the King — but say 'Father' to God. We are proud. How could it be otherwise when we say 'Brother' to his Son.

If you were different, you'd have misunderstood, you wouldn't be a member of this school — you wouldn't be a Christian.

22   WHO IS IN HEAVEN. Christ did not just bring us recipes for eternal life. He didn't come to teach us how we ought to live to win a happiness which only begins after death. So don't reduce his teaching to the command to collect merit points for heaven. You can't start finding joy in the next world. You can't start being happy in heaven.

We were created for happiness. Jesus wants to teach us how we should live in order to give others happiness and also to be happy ourselves here on earth. Eternal happiness is the continuation of a life like that.

81

23 THEY HAVE RECEIVED THEIR REWARD. First and foremost, watch your intentions. Watch especially the sources of your actions. Bear in mind the question 'why?': for what purpose, for what reason am I doing this or starting that?

Most of all look at your motives for what you do. This is where your greatness and baseness is decided, your humanity, your Christianity.

24 BLESSED ARE THE POOR, FOR THEIRS IS THE KINGDOM OF HEAVEN. A Christian cannot prosper. Can a Christian prosper if he loves his enemies, if he prays for those who persecute him and does good to those who injure him? If he gives to those who ask and does not turn away from those who want to borrow from him, if he gives his cloak to the person who has taken his coat, if his speech is simply 'Yes' and 'No'? If he searches for the kingdom of God and its righeousness and doesn't worry too much about what he is to eat or drink or wear.

And are you prospering?

25 'EPHPHATA', THAT IS, 'BE OPENED'. Who is a believer in Christ?

That woman in black who goes to church every day? The priest who celebrates the mass? The bearded religious in his habit and girdle? Or perhaps only the barefoot Carmelite monk separated from the world by his strict enclosure? Or the Trappist with his vow of perpetual silence?

Who is a believer in Christ today?

You are a woman, standing in front of the mirror in your new dress, combing your hair. You feel good because you think you look nice. Do you think that makes you a pagan?

And you are in love. You keep on dreaming of your girl, you long for her. Are you ashamed to raise your eyes to God?

And you in your turn are chatting with your colleague about ways of supplementing one's meagre pay with a part-time job. Do you think that separates you from your ideal of poverty of spirit? There were people who thought marriage was a sin, or condemned alcohol and even for the mass only used water, or

they insisted that all believers in Christ should sell all their possessions or distribute them to the poor and live in poverty.

But none of that was Christ's way — it was a blind alley.

26 IT WAS FITTING TO BE GLAD, FOR THIS YOUR BROTHER
WAS DEAD AND IS ALIVE. You are only a Christian if you can
forgive.

And you are only a Christian if — after your repentance — are
able to think of yourself as cleansed. As though you had not done
the evil, as though this sin had never existed in your life at all.
You are only a Christian if you really believe that you have been
forgiven, pardoned, that everything has been wiped out, that you
are being treated as a normal partner. And that, even if your sins
were red as scarlet, you have become whiter than snow.

27 AND HE WILL SEPARATE THEM ONE FROM ANOTHER. The
division will be made between those who have served a great
cause, a person, a human being, and those who only served their
own interests. The division will be made between those who
believed there was a point in devoting their lives to a cause or a
person and those who locked their lives inside themselves. The
division will be made without regard for which gods the people
believed in, which sanctuaries they went to, which denominations
they belonged to.

But this dividing line also runs through you, between, on the
one side, your striving to grab as much as possible for yourself,
to subordinate everything and everyone to your interests, and, on
the other, your openness to good, to his service, to sacrifice. The
division is taking place in you, here and now. You too will find
yourself on the one side or on the other in the next world according to the way you decide now. On the side you're on now.

28 DIVIDED AGAINST ITSELF. The division into believers and unbelievers doesn't just run on the other side of us.

The division into believers and unbelievers runs through each
of us, even you. You are the person who trembles for all his

possessions and wants to collect together as much as possible. And at the same time you are in the person who is able to be enthusiastic about beauty and to be pleased at every sign of goodness.

The division into believers and unbelievers goes through us — and you decide what you are.

29 SINNERS. If someone said you were a bad person you wouldn't believe it. If someone criticised you for acting dishonestly, you'd send them packing. If someone tried to persuade you that you needed to be converted, you'd laugh at them.

That is why the Church introduces you into the company of people like Nicodemus, Matthew, Peter and Magdalen, people like the Prodigal Son, the compassionate Samaritan. That is why the Church leads you to the light that is Jesus. So that without noticing you become transformed into a free, pure, big human being.

30 IF THEY PERSECUTED ME, THEY WILL PERSECUTE YOU. Do we follow him? Do we suffer for righteousness' sake? Do we serve God and not mammon? Are we persecuted for his name's sake? Are we the folly of this world? Do we keep on following him?

He went away alone to pray

1   WHEN YOU PRAY, GO INTO YOUR ROOM. Shut yourself in
your room. Turn the wick in the lamp down. Sit comfortably.
Lean your head back. Look at the Christmas tree, still glittering
in the corner, and try to sing Christmas carols. All by yourself —
for Jesus.

Learn to celebrate alone. Learn to live alone. Do not leave
everything to the crowd, the group, the society in which you
live. They can at most be a help to you, but in the last resort you
must act for yourself. No one in the end can make the decision
for you. No one, however much he wants to, however much he
loves you. You have to do it yourself.

Stay on your own and start singing carols. Listen to your
voice in the empty church of your room. You will feel as you did
the time you looked closely into the mirror and saw your other
face. Listen to yourself giving glory to God.

Learn to live alone. Not just in the crowd, not just in the
group, not just in society. This is just as important as the other.

2   IF ANYONE SHOULD THIRST. Jesus said that anyone who was
thirsty should come to him and drink. But who is not thirsty? He
said he didn't want to heal the healthy, but the sick. That he
hadn't come to call the just, but sinners. That the poor in spirit
were blessed.

So if you don't suffer from your sin, if you don't bump
against the cage of your finiteness, if you feel all right and have

made yourself comfortable, you don't need God.

But do you know for certain that this picture of you fits?

3 WHERE YOUR TREASURE IS. What eyes it must take to see such a pearl. What hands to lift such a treasure. With what eyes must one see, with what hands must one search, how must one experience such an overwhelming joy that for this one pearl, this one treasure, one can lightheartedly sell all that one has previously possessed, that one can lightheartedly give up everything that is not light, not purity.

4 THE KINGDOM OF HEAVEN IS AMONG YOU. All around us is another world. Within our reach. We belong to it, but it does not belong to us. From time to time grace comes like lightning and reveals it to one of us. Then that person who had the revelation tries to describe, in clumsy words, what he has experienced, what he has seen. Then we stare painfully at these words in an effort to find that world in them.

All around us is another world. We belong to it, but it does not belong to us.

5 SHUT THE DOOR AND PRAY TO YOUR FATHER WHO IS IN SECRET. You can feel God's presence when you pray, when you encounter human love, when you yourself make an effort to be good.

You can feel God's presence when you come across people whose lives are empty and lack it, when you are hurt by hatred and human wickedness.

You can feel God's presence when it is missing from your life, when you push it away through bad deeds — and this awareness hits you hardest.

6 THE GENTILES SEEK ALL THESE THINGS. From a distance you catch sight of people taking water out of the sea. You go closer and see that there are young people and old, men and

women. And then you look at their tortured faces, reddened with the effort, and suddenly your eye lights on the containers with which they are removing the water. You find to your horror that they are sieves.

'Father, you shouldn't be surprised that the children don't work in religion; they've got a lot to do. When we went to school, there wasn't so much to learn. But my child's coping; all his marks are good. That's the main thing".

'Oh yes, it's very important'.

'I didn't go to mass on Sunday. We went on an excursion. The departure was fixed for seven. In the end, though, we didn't leave till eight, but how were we to know? We got back quite late'.

'I can't manage to say a prayer in the mornings. You're hardly up before work starts. And in the evening you're so tired. You put your head on the pillow and you're asleep straight away'.

The exhausted, the restless, the overworked — they draw water with sieves.

7   PRAY. You won't find any medicine against cancer for your child. You won't protect it from loneliness or save it from despair. Teach it to live with God. So that it will be in his company on walks and at school, so that it judges the value of life in his company, of life, entertainment, politics, books, people and itself.

The place to learn this is prayer. That is why one should take the greatest care, and think carefully about the child's soul, and choose only the simplest words or put them together with the child. The further his spiritual development advances, the more help must be given to deepen the young person's religious experience.

You won't find any medicine to cure your cancer. You won't protect yourself against loneliness or save yourself from despair. Learn to live with God.

8   OUR DAILY BREAD. Perhaps God will appear to you too in the burning bush. Perhaps you too will hear, in the middle of ordinary

activities, the words, 'The ground on which you are standing is holy'. All your doing are holy — they are meant to be holy. Later everything returns to its original state, and everyday human things and activities become central once more. But don't let this transfiguration be taken from you. This is one of the greatest graces a human being can be given, the realization that his life is holy.

9   YOUR PROPHETS. Each of us has something of the prophet in him. God reveals himself to everyone in an unrepeatable way; it is given to everyone to see God, the world, people and himself in some form of truth. Each of us must have something of the prophet about him. Each of us must pass on to people what he has seen, must share with them what he has been given.

If you let that go, you will become like a bureaucrat, stamping other people's ideas.

10   THEY SAW NO ONE BUT JESUS ONLY. Transfigure yourself before us. Show yourself to us in all your brightness and all your greatness. Make us fascinated by you like Peter, James and John. Make us receive something of your glory as we look on you.

Transfigure us, transform us. We do not know what we ask for. We do not know the heights to which you can lead us. We do not know what vistas you can show us. We do not know what powers you can awaken in us.

We can feel our lives running away into nothing, as we look round ever more vigorously for a comfortable armchair, as we long more and more for complete peace at any price. Transform us. Take us out of ourselves — we can still bear it. While there is time. The day is turning, and our sun is already going down.

11   HE WAS TRANSFIGURED BEFORE THEM. It is impossible to live in constant ecstasy and rapture. It comes like the light of a lighthouse; it shines out briefly and then falls back into darkness. And you don't know when it will shine out next.

So, when you receive the grace of illumination and see the

truth, fix it fast in the iron frame of resolutions; draw from it the full consequences for everyday life, to keep it safe through the period of defeats, failures, disappointment, struggles with your own pettiness, cowardice, idleness — so that it enriches your life permanently.

12 WHO SAYS, 'LORD, LORD'. How hard it is to come down from the mount of transfiguration, to drop down to earth the eyes which had been raised to heaven, to unravel the knots of earthly problems with hands accustomed to the gestures of prayer.

How hard it is to come down from the mount of transfiguration. The nicest thing would be to stay up there — or perhaps not to go up at all?

13 ALL THE DAYS. Even though the person you love treats you with contempt, even though your friends abandon you, even though your followers stop believing in you, even though people laugh at you and you are thrown on the roadside like a human rag, he will never leave you alone. He will come to you as he came to the mother of the young man of Nain, to the woman who was a sinner, to Zacchaeus, and will say to you quite simply, 'Do not weep', 'Your sins are forgiven', 'I must stay at your house today'. He will come like the Samaritan to the man who lay by the roadside. He will pour wine and oil on the wounds, put you on his beast and bring you to a safe place.

14 YOU SHALL FIND REST. In your loneliness and pain, when you miss the touch of a human hand to lift you up, calm you, soothe you, show sympathy . . . In your loneliness and your pain, when no one is able to free you, support you, comfort you — you will always find him.

15 DO THIS IN REMEMBRANCE OF ME. We are a community which believes in Christ. We celebrate the anniversary of his birth, his torment and resurrection. We celebrate this because we

remember; we celebrate because we want to think of him. Every such anniversary brings him before our eyes with the injunction, 'Look what he was like — your master and lord. And you?' And each of these anniversaries is meant to lead us to greatness, to confidence, to courage, to forgiveness, to peace — to humanity.

16   THE BLOOD OF THE COVENANT, WHICH IS POURED OUT FOR MANY FOR THE FORGIVENESS OF SINS. That is the holiest prayer a human being could compose. The greatest sacrifice one human being could offer another. The most beautiful thank-you a human being could ever say to God.

The holy mass can be your prayer, your sacrifice, your thanksgiving.

17   FREE SONS. The church is the place where you should feel free. Here no one has the right to enslave you. Here you have no need to lie or put on an act. Here you do not come before a court, but before him who wants your good, in spite of everything and at all costs. You are before him whom you do not need to fear.

18   HE WHO EATS MY FLESH AND DRINKS MY BLOOD. But perhaps churches are too beautiful, tabernacles too ornate, the liturgy too elaborate, church language too baroque, the hierarchy too pompous. And we have forgotten that *we* are the temple of the holy spirit, that *we* are the chosen people, the holy people, the royal priesthood, that God lives in *us*.

19   I DESIRE MERCY AND NOT SACRIFICES. In our temples there is no altar with a fire burning on it. We do not make burnt offerings. We know: God desires 'mercy and not sacrifices'. We know: even if we gave him all our wealth, it would be no use. God wants us.

If this is so, and if you don't want to forget it, offer him small sacrifices. Not just abstinence on Friday, not just the Sunday money offerings, not just candles in front of the altar or flowers, but the little awkwardnesses the day brings with it, your little readiness for sacrifice, for which the needy stretch out their hands.

20   THAT BELIEVING YOU MAY HAVE LIFE. How can we believe when there are so many egoists all round us?

How can we have confidence, when so many people are giving up all round us?

How can we love when there are so many hard hearts all round us?

How can we believe, trust and love, when in ourselves there is so much distrust, unbelief, so much lack of love? Isn't it easier to turn our backs on this disorder, make money, look after our own affairs, bother about our own health?

If we don't do that, it is because, though it is an invisible flame, it shows us the way, because, though it is only a crumb, it does not let us starve — because it is the most precious thing in us.

And so, torn this way and that between belief and unbelief, between trust and distrust, between love and its lack, we gather round the altar to learn to live from him who gave his life for the truth.

21   REMEMBER THE SABBATH DAY, TO KEEP IT HOLY. You must not let yourself be possessed. No thing — not even the holiest, no person, even the holiest, should consume you totally. You must not give yourself totally even to the greatest cause, even to the greatest person. Neither work nor love, not loss, not victory, not defeat, not mistakes should take possession of you.

And so you must celebrate. This is the only salvation from the danger that constantly threatens you. So you must celebrate, must disengage even from these greatest of affairs, go away even from these greatest of people — in order to get at a distance from yourself and all your affairs in the perspective of absolute goodness, truth and beauty. You must put them in their proper place according to their worth.

That is why the ability to celebrate is as important as work.

22   HE WITHDREW TO A LONELY PLACE. Throw a blanket over your shoulder, take your swimming things in your hand and a book under your arm — but one you enjoy — put on your sunglasses, take something light to cover your head, and go on to the beach. Spread the blanket out, lie down and try not to think of anything.

Oh yes, before that put a stick in the sand beside the blanket and hang the white towel on it. As a sign that you're giving in. You know that lots of your affairs are unfinished, but all that is now going to stop bothering you. You'll see to it when your holiday is over.

All that won't be so easy. In the first few days it will irritate you every minute: you didn't get this or that done, you have to tell someone something, give something to some one else and get something from a third. Hold on tight to the blanket, and when it gets on your nerves, look at your flag and remind yourself: you've given in.

Maybe God will grant that you hear the sea and the wood rustle, maybe you will discover that the clouds are gliding across the sky, and notice that the birds are singing and the grass is green.

23   THE FEAST DREW NEAR. You cannot always be going around in an apron, a white coat, an overall or training suit. You can't be a person whose only source of interest, amusement, and activity is work — no matter how involved in it you are. You must have time for something which isn't work. And not relaxation, but celebration.

Be a guest. When someone asks you to a party, go. And don't behave as though you were at work. Don't be in a hurry. Don't eat to fill yourself. Don't drink to quench your thirst, but to celebrate.

Be a host. Throw your house open. Send invitations to your parties. Let your home — this machine for eating, sleeping and working — be transformed into a banqueting hall. Prepare a special meal. Enjoy yourself. Not to achieve anything, but to get back to general human problems, which affect you as well as others.

Celebrate, be human.

24 IN THE GLORY OF HIS FATHER. We and our hymns. We and
our silk vestments and our jewelled chalices, in churches strewn
with gold. We and all our ceremonies, songs and celebrations.

Isn't the mass a commemoration of Jesus' suffering and death?
So why so much gold, colour, light and music?

Because Christ is not just the man of sorrows, but also the
risen one, who will sit in the glory of his Father.

Because the mass is not just a commemoration of Jesus'
suffering and death, but also a participation in the glory of God.
Because we are not just burdened with work in the service of man,
but already here and now — through a life like this — share in
God's glory.

That is why we celebrate like this, and this celebration is a
symbol of the glory which will be fully relevant to us in the life
to come.

25 REST A LITTLE. Have a good rest during the holidays.

See how green the grass is, how blue the sky, how white clouds
move across the sky. Go along the path between the fields ruffled
by the wind. Stretch out by the side of the sea and listen to its
roar.

Perhaps you want to spend this time in a different way. Good.
The only important thing is that you get back to yourself, re-
discover your rhythm and look calmly at yourself again, at yourself, at other people, work and the world — that you should feel
free again.

26 ON THE HOLY DAY. The tools have been cleared away, the
machines turned off, the drawing boards covered. The work-
shops are silent, the offices empty, no telephones ring.

We don't just exist to do jobs and work. We don't exist just to
do physical and intellectual work, to write and do calculations, to
get things done, shopping, washing, tidying, to rush.

27 I DESIRE MERCY, AND NOT SACRIFICE. We don't live to go to
church. But we do go to church in order to live like human beings.

93

But people do distinguish us from others by the fact that we go to church on Sundays. Ultimately, though, it ought to be different: 'By this all men will know that you are my disciples, if you have love for one another'.

28 MY CHURCH. All that the Church is and all its manifestations has only one aim. The sacraments and the eucharist, the liturgy with its vast diversity of services, rites, processions, dedications, in the rhythm of the liturgical year from Advent to the descent of the holy spirit, the hierarchy from the chaplains through the prelates and cardinals to the pope; all that we call the teaching of the Church, including both simple preaching and the probing analyses of theologians; church art with all its riches of music, vestments, vessels, architecture, painting, sculpture, church decoration — all that the Church is and all its manifestations has only one aim: that you may believe more, trust more, love more.

29 BUT WE HAVE A HOPE. There is a time of people like Judas, who sell Jesus, of people like Peter, who deny him before a maid, of people like Thomas, who keep on saying they won't believe unless they see him; a time of the disappointed disciples on the way to Emmaus. That is the time of the calculating, the careful, the frightened, the idle. And even then you can meet him. Once more, perhaps for the last time, he puts himself in our path, to ask: 'Where are you going?'

30 FOLLOW ME. Jesus revealed himself to Peter on a different road, on a different road to Zacchaeus, on a different road to Magdalen, on a different road again to Nicodemus, on a different road to you. And not just once. For example, he revealed himself to Peter after the miraculous catch of fish, in the courtyard of the high priest's palace, and after the resurrection on the shore of the lake.

Christianity is not a uniform that you put on. Christianity is Christ who steps into your path or whom you go out to meet.

31 THE SABBATH WAS MADE FOR MAN. What a good thing it is
that we have Advent, Christmas, Lent, Easter and Sunday. What a
good thing it is that we respect these institutions and subordinate
ourselves to their rhythm in spite of all our idleness, in spite of
our moods, in spite of striving for spontaneity, unrestrained
freedom and novelty. And on Sunday we go to Church to mass
and refrain from heavy work, on Friday we keep abstinence, in
winter we celebrate the anniversary of Christ's birth, in spring
that of his passion and resurrection, in summer the day of the
descent of the holy Spirit.

What a good thing it is that we have erected the feast days
along the road of our life to pull us out of our pettiness.

August

The measure of love

1   ONLY ONE THING IS NECESSARY. Too many people, too many duties, too many worries, too many years.

Too little time, too little money, too little patience. Too little love.

2   THOU SHALT LOVE THE LORD THY GOD. You will only see yourself in full light, when you find your place, when you discover that he treats you as a person, is interested in you, loves you, is glad that you are here and are you; that he accepts everything that goes with you, even if it is a long way from perfection, that he is understanding about your failings, if you can at least bring yourself to make a gesture of contrition.

You will not be able to give all that is in you until you become fond of him, until it becomes important to you not to let yourself down in his sight, not to let him down, until only his opinion of you is important to you.

3   WHICH IS THE GREATEST COMMANDMENT? Do you still believe in love? Do you believe that there can be a person in the world who can do something for your sake and not just for their own benefit? Do you believe in love — that you too can live a selfless life, can exist for another person, not just for yourself?

I ask you about this all the more the older you are, the more you've burnt your fingers on people and on yourself. The more you have seen through all the well-turned phrases, each sweet smile, each piece of friendliness, all the presents and the good turns — which you see as all pretence, covering nothing but self-interest.

But you cannot but believe in it. In the end a selfless life like that is the basis of your humanity — of your redemption.

4 FOR SHE LOVED MUCH. Have you ever in your life said, 'How nice to see you', 'How nice that you came, rang up, got in touch'? Have you even once in your life been keen about something and stopped being alone, stopped being afraid: of the world, people, yourself, of your illness, your death. Have you been happy at least once in your life?

But maybe once in your life you have experienced something more. Perhaps you have felt eyes on you saying 'How nice to see you'. Perhaps you have not only loved, but been loved.

And do you love someone now? Are you still loved? Don't say those times are over. Times can always be wonderful. It just all depends on you. Look around you with the same freshness as in the past. Then you will discover delightful people and see really important things.

5 IF YOU BELIEVE. We have no idea how much we depend on the world, how much we are a part of its biology, intertwined with its matter; how far we are a part of the society in which we live, how we think in its categories, succumb to its ideologies, react with its reflexes, breathe with its rhythm.

We do not realize how much fear of death leaves a mark on our actions; how far death is the source of our failings: when we make use of others to protect ourselves, when we destroy competitiors to improve our own chances, when we use every means to collect material goods.

That is why every good deed takes on such importance. That is why it is so difficult to give oneself, to forgive, to trust, to love. It is always a step in the dark, a risk of reducing oneself, destroying oneself, coming closer to death.

6   YOUR FRIENDS. We meet and part again.

Small acts of politeness, courtesies, mutual favours, warmth, sympathy, close contacts, friendships, instances of sacrifice. Then there is usually either a formal farewell or a gradual separation. Previous friendships are replaced by new ones, and new obligations are created; you tire youself out for someone else, sacrifice yourself for them.

The current of love. Sometimes it runs deep down, hardly perceptible, sometimes it comes to the surface and becomes the main content of life. But it must always be present. Its absence means the death of the soul. What we prosaically call selfishness.

7   THOU SHALT LOVE THY NEIGHBOUR. If you prefer to be on first-name terms with everyone you will always be lonely. If you want to be friends with all the world, you'll have no friends. If you want to be in love with everyone, you won't really love anyone.

8   ALONE. Don't push away the hand that smooths your scarf, strokes your hair and brushes the dust off your coat. Don't get upset when people ask you how you're feeling, whether you have a headache, if you've got a cold, how you slept, whether anything's bothering you. Don't complain that people are interested in you and interfering in your affairs. Don't complain that people give you advice, warn you, try to convince you. There will come a time when nobody's interested in you, when nobody asks you questions or warns you or asks you for things. It will be as you wanted: no one will bother with you. You will be left alone. And then when the tragedy comes the hand that might save you from despair may be missing.

Don't push love away; it isn't always around.

9   SHE SAT AT THE LORD'S FEET AND LISTENED TO HIS TEACHING. Do you love anyone? Is there a person you long for, one you admire and revere, for whom you do hundreds of incredible things, just to give him or her pleasure? Someone for

whose every word and every smile you are always grateful, of whom you always feel unworthy, whom you always want to be with to receive some of their light? Do you love someone?

Don't you love anyone any more? You're like an extinct volcano. Sometimes you touch the cold lava with a suspicious hand, look with surprised eyes at its fantastic forms and ask in amazement, 'Was that me, I who now am only worried about my own welfare'?

10 THIS IS THE GREAT AND FIRST COMMANDMENT. Giving, borrowing, going with, meeting, visiting, helping, protecting, doing things for — giving your money, your time, yourself. Not so that they will later repay you, visit you, go to meet you, help you, protect you, do things for you; not so that they'll thank you, reward you, give you their money, their time, themselves. But because that's how it must be and ought not to be otherwise — for the sake of moral duty, of honesty, justice, truth, beauty and goodness. That is true love.

11 GIVE AND IT WILL BE GIVEN TO YOU. When you give you will receive. Avarice, greed and envy shut you up in yourself. When you want to keep everything, when you don't want to share, so that others can't learn from you, so that others can't become equal with you — then not only do you shut yourself off from them but also them from you.

When you give, you open yourself to others. And only then will you receive.

12 LEST THE LIGHT IN YOU BE DARKNESS. Don't be surprised if words reach you that you never spoke, actions that you never performed. Don't complain if people are constantly whispering behind your back, attributing evil deeds to you and implying bad intentions. That is the price of your freedom. The price for being someone. In the face of their own muddled lives they envy your ability to think, your lack of fear of plain speech, your ability to act. They can't forgive you your good fortune. They can't stand

you because you give them pangs of conscience.

But you be careful too. If anxiety, grief and anger spring up in your soul because someone else's life is a success, because someone is free and creative. Either you'll want to kill that light so that it becomes darkness like yourself or you'll fan it to make it shine brighter. Then there is a chance that your light will start to shine.

13   IN WHOM IS NO GUILE. What is concealed behind their polite greetings, smiling faces, friendly words and courtesies? How do they really think about you? As an enemy or as a friend?

What is concealed behind your warmth, your politeness? How do you really regard the people you work with, your superiors, your subordinates? As enemies or friends? Do you strive to get them out of the way, or do you want to be a help to them in their lives?

We have learnt the art of deception so well that we are no longer able to guess people's attitudes to us, so well that we are no longer able to guess who we are.

14   BE IT DONE TO YOU AS YOU DESIRE. It depends on you whether you get lonely.

You decide yourself whether you are necessary to others. You yourself cut yourself out of their lives, and only you can rejoin them.

Another person can help you, through kindness. In just the same way you can pull someone out of the banishment of his loneliness, by showing him kindness.

15   FRIENDS. I would hope that you could have one person who would not betray you even if he could do well for himself out of it. Someone you could walk along beside happily, without being afraid he'd push you into the ditch. Someone you could happily let go on in front of you in the knowledge that he wouldn't block the road. Someone you could happily have behind you without fear that he'd stick a knife in your back. I would like you to have

a person who in return for this loyalty to you wouldn't have designs on your freedom or on your free time – or on you.

I would hope that you wouldn't betray your friend even if you could do well for yourself out of it . . . That in return for this loyal behaviour you wouldn't demand an exclusive place in his life, in his thoughts, in his time. That you wouldn't take him over as though he were your property.

16 IF YOU ONLY LOVE THOSE WHO LOVE YOU. You can't live in the shell of your loneliness. You need to have your actions checked by people around you, need acceptance or rebuke, a handshake, a greeting, a smile, a kind word, recognition, admiration or not – so long as it's not indifference. Look, beside you someone on the edge of despair is shouting, 'I'm here! I'm here!' And while he looks around helplessly he is waiting for an answer, but all that reaches him is the echo of his own cry. Watch him.

17 THAT THEY MAY BE ONE. We are like communicating pipes. We are like sources of light. We are like sources of heat. Together we strengthen each other by good, and suffocate each other by evil. On your holiness therefore depends the holiness of the people connected with you: your friends, children, subordinates, colleagues, pupils.

How strong is the light in you? How large the circle of people who draw on your warmth? Does it include the dead?

You want to be convinced of your greatness? Look at the people who live alongside you.

18 BY THIS WILL THEY KNOW THAT YOU ARE MY BROTHERS. What do you know of your neighbours on the other side of the wall? That they sometimes put the radio or television on too long? That they celebrate their birthdays with a great deal of noise? Do you say hello to each other? Have you ever visited them? Ever invited them to visit you? Did you ever keep an eye on their children or bring them meals when they were sick, or lend them food or money. Are you interested in the people

who live beside you? Are you a Christian?

19   WHO SEES IN SECRET. The measure of our faith is that marginal area of our activity for which no one pays us, not with money or a good turn or with gratitude. The measure of our faith is the marginal area of good deeds about which no one knows. The measure of our faith is our humanity.

Otherwise we are like the Pharisees who gave alms at street-corners in order to be seen.

20   THE OWNER. Beware of misusing love. Whether it is a boy-friend or girl-friend, husband or wife, parent or child, you will be tempted to turn the loved person into your property. You want to know about every step he takes, to get to know all his friends, keep an eye on his work and leisure, be with him all the time, never let him out of your sight, question him, trail him. You want to have him just for your own interests and problems, fill him totally with yourself, so that he has no time left for independent thought, for initiatives of his own, for a personal life. You want to bind him to you with requests, pleas and warnings, make him dependent on your decisions, subordinate him to your life, force your model on to him and your views about big and small things alike, form him in your image, by force or tricks make his ideas and reactions follow your pattern.

Until finally you know every question and answer, every reaction and every thought. And that's the end. Not the end of love, since that will be long gone. Just boredom. And then you'll go away. Unless the person who loved you a long time ago has previously been able to escape, to save his freedom and personality.

21   A MAN'S FOES WILL BE THOSE OF HIS OWN HOUSEHOLD. You know your wife's dresses, skirts and blouses exactly. You know the face she makes when she combs her hair in the morning in front of the mirror or when she puts on her make-up before she goes into town. You know her turns of phrase and what she thinks of the neighbours. And it all irritates you more and more. Until you suddenly find that someone is interested in her, has even fallen in love with her. That astounds you. In love with her? With what? With her down-at-heel slippers, her strikingly ugly ears, her tattered apron-strings? After all, you know her best.

No, you don't know her. You were certainly nearer the truth when you first saw her.

22   GIVE AN ACCOUNT. Why is it so easy to tell a married couple from an unmarried couple — in the street, in a train or in the cinema? Because in marriage there is no longer any danger of separation? Because when you left the altar you left the task of preserving love entirely to God, because you thought the sacrament gave you an eternal guarantee?

Why do you only bother about your appearance when you go out? Why do you only smile and become able to chat so fascinatingly when there are visitors?

Love in marriage can't be kept alive in a dirty dressing-gown and with uncombed hair. It can't be protected with an unshaven chin, or with jealousy and scenes.

If every love is a flower, so is love in marriage, but, like any other love it is not immortal. If love is a swallow, it is a living swallow, not a specimen under glass. A real, live swallow. You have to take care that it doesn't fly away.

23   FOR THEY SHALL SEE GOD. We have destroyed the taboo of sexuality. We have said and revealed everything in human physiology and psychology. We have removed the mystery of marriage. We have laughed at virginity, celibacy and married love. There is nothing in this area of life which has not been mocked.

And still we are tormented by the anxiety that we have let go of something very important. Something essential to our humanity: we have less and less idea what love is.

24   HE SAID TO THE INNKEEPER, 'TAKE CARE OF HIM'. We even tend to play the part of the Samaritan and pick up a person

we don't like, tend his wounds and give him into the care of an innkeeper, leaving money as well, and a promise that we'll come back.

More often, though, we find ourselves in the part of the inn-keeper: God has left a poor person on our doorstep for us to look after. We can also keep the door closed.

25   MOVED WITH PITY. Christian love is not some obstinate activity. Christian love cannot be something you force on the world, not an attitude with which you want to make other people happy.

Christian love is true love, that is attentiveness and openess to everything happening around you. Only this openness — once you have seen its necessity — produces the deed, of warding off evil or helping. But first come the attentiveness and openness you bring to your surroundings. Otherwise you only injure people with an act on which you stick the label of Christian love.

26   IF YOU HAVE LOVE. Each of us is different. Each of us has different gifts, different views, opinions and habits, a different life-style. Each of us embodies a different world. This means that collisions are inevitable, about trivialities and essentials. That is normal. Abnormality begins where the desire for exclusiveness takes hold of you — the desire to dominate your opponent, to destroy those who are different, to make your world system binding on everyone.

It is easier to be indulgent towards a weakness, a failing, help-lessness and vices. But to recognize a talent, to tolerate it, not to obstruct it, actually to support it, collaborate with it, help it to develop, admire it — that is no longer justice, but heroism.

27   WOE TO YOU. Don't let yourself be shouted at. Ask for the reasons, the justification, the validity. Ask whether the other side doesn't bear some responsibility. And even if, frightened by the shouting, you cower and can't get a word out, then at least keep quite — don't start beating your breast and apologising.

Don't let yourself be shouted at — unless it comes from love.

Then even a telling off can bring you pleasure.

Don't scream yourself. Even when you're in the right. Shouting is inhuman. Don't shout at people. You have no right to. It torments them. Even if they listen, it is with hatred, because you've trampled on their human dignity — because you've injured them.

Don't shout at people — unless it comes from love. Love always includes pleasure.

28   GIVE. The most precious thing to anyone is time. We are never so anxious about anything as about time. And there is nothing we are so sparing to others of as time. Nor is there any greater gift we can give another person than time. To devote our time to another person means to try to listen to what he is really saying, to understand him, to help him — to share in his life.

The measure of a person's cleverness is the way he organizes their time. A measure of love is how he gives his time to other people.

29   MAN DOES NOT LIVE BY BREAD ALONE. You cannot live on a kind word for a moment, an hour, two hours or a whole day. A kind word can save you in a moment of despair. It is hard to live without a kind word. So don't be ashamed that someone has praised you, don't despise a kind word. Don't be afraid it may turn your head — after all, enough unkind words come down on you every day.

You can live a long time on a kind word, so give people one when they deserve it. They need to be accepted by their fellow men, otherwise life is difficult. Don't be afraid it may turn their heads. They get their daily share of unkind words, not just from others, but from you too.

30   THEY SAID TO HIM, 'THEY ARE ALL LOOKING FOR YOU'. You will be important as long as you work for the *cause*. The more you commit yourself to it, the more people will follow you, without sparing time or money. But they will all go away as soon

as you make the cause a source of profit for you. If anyone stays with you then, it will only be out of sympathy and in the hope of your repentance.

31   GREAT CROWDS FOLLOWED HIM. We can't stand the crowd. We are unable to embrace the people who push their way to us from all sides. We are not able to take on their suffering all round us. Even if you wept the whole day, you couldn't weep away the whole of human misfortune. Even if you helped people your whole life long, it would only be a drop in the ocean of human distress. Even if your heart went out to all the lonely, how many people could you give it to? Ten, a hundred, a thousand? And what about the rest?

We can't stand the mass. We stand there, terrorized by the abundance of human sorrow. We put down the visor, slip into our armour to defend ourselves, to hold out, to live. Coldbloodedly we organize people into categories: passers-by, dealers, officials, customers, acquaintances. Lonely and inaccessible, we look blankly at all of them and go through life like that. Without being surprised at anything, without resenting anyone.

Why live?

According to the measure of the grace God has given you, according to the largeness of your heart and your feeling, embrace with your love all who come to you.

September

Hope transforms everything

1   HE KNOWS. I don't know how God has ordained the rest of your life, nor do you. That is not our business. What is important is that you should know he has prepared it for you. What is important is that you should know that he will always be with you; he is banking on you just as he wants you to bank on him.

2   FEAR AND TERROR HAD SEIZED THEM. Yes. Nobody asked you if you wanted to be alive. Nobody asked you whether, assuming you did, you were happy with this sort of life. Do you want to live, with the spectre of death before you? Maybe you even say, 'If I had known that my life would turn out like this, I would have preferred not to live'.

In reality, however, you had no choice. Don't complain then, to yourself and others, that your parents didn't guide you properly and you had a boring childhood. That you came across people who interfered with your development. That people treated you badly and you were ill. Don't keep complaining.

It is your fate. You must accept it and bear it with dignity. It was given to you by him who loves you.

3   I MUST STAY AT YOUR HOUSE TODAY. Pay attention to your present. Don't look backwards — except to draw conclusions from the defeats you have suffered and the successes you have achieved. Don't gaze into the future — except insofar

as you need so not to lose your way. Your present should be as plain as possible, should be absolutely honest; treat it with great seriousness. It determines you; it confirms or erases your past. It sets the direction of your future through your decision here and now.

Behind you the curtain of the past has already fallen. In front of you is uncertainty. Concentrate on your present.

4 YOUR TIME. Don't stare at your past as if you were hypnotized. You will be more and more horrified as you see how many opportunities and chances you missed — they are gone beyond recall. Don't state back at the past or fresh possibilities and chances will slip through your fingers which you must seize immediately — you mustn't let them go. Otherwise in a year, oerhaps even after a few hours, you'll mourn this past time.

Don't stare back at your past, but take what God is putting into your hand now.

5 HE WENT AWAY SORROWFUL FOR HE HAD GREAT POSSESSIONS. If only you could stop being afraid once in your life. If only for once in your life you were not concerned what people said about you. If only for once in your life you could manage not to worry about money, but involve yourself totally in a cause. At least once in your life begin, quite unselfishly, to help someone. At least once in your life get enthusiastic. At least once in your life. . .

Ever after you'll long for that time. You'll never again be satisfied with your slyness and rapacity. No matter what positions of power you obtain, however much money you amass.

Be free at least once in your life. Then you'll always long for that sort of life.

6 DO NOT BE FRIGHTENED. Don't start being frightened, or you'll never stop. Don't soothe yourself with the thought that you just want to get your life a bit more stable, wait till the storm blows over, and then you'll stop being frightened. It's not true.

The more you rise, the more you have, the more will fear increase in you, for all you've achieved, for all your loved ones and for yourself. . . . .

Don't be frightened. Don't live in fear. What do you get out of a life like that? God created us for happiness.

7   IF GOD SO CLOTHES THE GRASS OF THE FIELD, WILL HE NOT MUCH MORE CLOTHE YOU, O MEN OF LITTLE FAITH? Do not fear the present or the past or the future, either other people or the world, either questions or answers, either letters or telegrams, either colleagues or superiors.

Don't let yourself be frightened when you dream at night of disasters, illness and human jealousy. Step fearlessly out into the new day.

Depend on it: both you and the world you fear so much are in his hand. Depend on it with all your heart, in spite of the panic which grows in you and in spite of the pressure you think you feel from outside. God sees better than your eyes can.

8   HAVE CONFIDENCE. What do you think of yourself? That you're brilliant? Very intelligent? What is left of your 'dreams of power'? And of your youthful dreams of greatness? The extinguished eyes of a person who seeks only his modest existence and quiet.

But there are still potentialities in you that you cannot even feel. You are capable of deeds you never thought of in your wildest dreams. Greatness slumbers within you.

9   WHO BETRAYED HIM. Have confidence in yourself. Have confidence that you can be honest, that you can behave with dignity, that you won't become a traitor, a coward or vulgar, that you'll measure up to your responsibilities, carry out the tasks given you, that you are capable of love and loyalty. Have confidence in yourself.

Have confidence in other people. Trust that they won't leave you alone, that they'll keep faith with you, won't leave you alone when you're sick, will help you, understand you, that they'll see their mistake.

Have confidence in another person. Have confidence in yourself.

And even if you've deceived yourself, think: 'This is an isolated instance which shouldn't destroy your confidence'.

10   YOU WHO LABOUR AND ARE HEAVY LADEN. You wanted to win a lot of money. With all the shyness of your eight years you went up to the machine. You put in the first coin, still warm from your trembling hand. The numbers began to move, you pressed 'start' or 'stop', but in vain. You put in the second coin, then the third, and finally the last. At some point — you still remember, even though it's so long ago — your father said you'd never get anywhere. You still remember very clearly. Once a friend gave you a good thrashing, and as you ran home crying, yelled a word after you which hurt more than the hardest thump.

And later you missed out on the great love. You really did. You carefully put together the words you wanted to say, you planned a meeting. You even wrote a long letter, but in the end it never got sent. Recently you found out that she loved you too, but she didn't dare admit it to you.

You look around and find that so many of your old classmates who are neither more gifted nor more honest than you are now in good position while you're stuck hopelessly in the same rut with no chance of getting any further.

You feel as you did when you went away from the machine. You had problems from the start, and it'll be like that till the end of your life.

Is your dream, what you'd given up everything else for, to begin life all over again: 'Now I'd know how I ought to live'?

Would you believe that this is every person's dream?

11   THE SPIRIT BLOWS WHERE HE WILL. Don't close the doors and windows. Don't wait for the time of your youth to come back. Don't think that the reality of the present will pass like a dream, will roll back like a wave. Don't say that the only honest people belong to the past, that only the literature, poetry and art

of the past was worth anything. And don't try to underpin such a position with your Catholicism. There is no Catholic goodness, Catholic truth, Catholic beauty. All goodness is from God, from Christ. The same applies to beauty and truth, even if they bear the sign of another religion, another world view. Open wide the doors and windows. Be objective. Don't be afraid to admit that others are right, to recognize and adopt things. Don't be afraid to be pleased about people who work beside you, about their various successes — even if these people don't believe in God.

12 CONSIDER THE LILIES OF THE FIELD. Don't start your reading of the newspaprer with the obituaries and the war reports. Don't be frightened by the statistics of deaths from cancer and heart diseases. Don't let yourself get worked up by circulars, company reports and balances. Or depressed by obligations, functions and urgent business. Don't complain that you can't believe any longer in human honesty and kindness. Don't say your life's over now, and you don't expect anything more out of it. Just lift up your head and you'll feel the spring wind on your face, you'll see how much light there is around you.

Depend on it; what's in store for you is far richer than you expect.

13 HAVE CONFIDENCE. It gets more and more difficult to wake up quickly, to disentangle oneself from the trightening dreams. The screams of the sirens are more and more threatening. Increasingly we are submerged in circulars, regulations, and reminders. The pile of obligations, functions, unfinished things grows to ever more frightening proportions over our heads. In the papers we find more and more reports from battlefields, reports of failures, statistics of motor accidents and incurable diseases. Memories from our childhood become more and more frequent. We have less and less hope that anything extraordinary will happen in our lives now, that we might stilly prosper, that we will be happy — so many years have passed meaninglessly, and in us there is a growing belief in our own old age and our own death.

113

But here we must have confidence, boundless confidence in God about everything.

14 EVERYTHING IS A GIFT. Don't be always on the look-out for other people's happiness. Remove from your mind words like, 'He is successful'. With that attitude you'll always be unhappy, whatever you achieve. In fact, you know, it's not like that. Everything you are and possess, your whole life, each of your days with all that it brings, is a gift. Recognize this gift. Accept it, appreciate it and be grateful.

15 EVEN THE HAIRS OF YOUR HEAD ARE ALL NUMBERED. It's not true that you've got problems and everything in your life is going wrong. Don't give yourself up to the illusion that you need optimum conditions to develop all your possibilities without hindrance and not have to spend time or energy on wandering around, coming back to the same spot, making sure you have the bare essentials of life.

Don't think that fate has a grudge against you or that you must have a comfortable environment to develop in. It is precisely these unfavourable conditions, they above all, which allow your humanity to develop fully.

16 THOSE WHO WEEP. Don't hang around your failures. Don't let pity for yourself affect you. If you do, you'll easily remember how sad your childhood was, how dull your youth was. You'll have no trouble finding a whole series of sorrows in your life. You'll complain how unhappy and how poor you are. Every subsequent defeat will only worsen this situation.

You'll only be able to save yourself if you can free yourself from yourself and see at least one other person besides yourself. You'll find that they suffer too. You'll see that everyone suffers, not just you.

17 HE WHO PERSEVERES TO THE END. Human life consists in

large part of defeats, only to a small extent of successes. And
there would be no successes if the defeats didn't exist. That is
why it is so important to learn how to accept defeats, lack of
results, gossip, negative judgments and lack of recognition. That
is why it is so important to persevere, to sort oneself out in the
new situation, to organize one's disrupted plans, to wait and start
again.

18   LIKE THE OTHERS. Don't wait for the prince to come and carry
you off like Cinderella.

Don't wait around listening for the knock at the door which
will bring you out of hiding and present you to the world as a
newly discovered talent.

You are not the best mother or the best father, not the best
wife or the best husband, not the best daughter or the best son,
not the best nurse, teacher or office-worker. Not just you, no;
nobody is, because everyone is only human. If someone draws
your attention to something, marks up a failure against you, it's
no reason for the world to disintegrate before your eyes because
someone could say something like that to you. Not just to you —
everyone can be criticized for something.

Don't keep wanting to be unique. God made many different
flowers in the field. It would be bad if one of them were to re-
place all the others. You have to be different.

19   YOUR FATHER KNOWS WHAT YOU NEED. When you are
very happy and full of joy, if you feel great satisfaction, the
feeling of having done something well from first to last, and if
you can't in the least imagine anything threatening you — then
usually some blow falls. Suddenly, and from a side from which
you least expected it.

But the blow comes from the same hand as the previous gift.

20   THE DAYS SHALL COME UPON YOU. Perhaps you no longer
ask 'Why?' with the startled eyes of a child whom someone has
suddenly smacked. Now if some joy comes into your life, you

know straight away that you'll be getting the bill, a sorrow. Perhaps you've even noticed something more, that life is subject to a law of series. There are times when everything is wonderful, when the grass is green, the sky is blue, the sun is shining, the mist charming. People are kind. Everything goes according to plan, you have no doubt about the value of life. Then comes the bill: bad days full of sorrow. Then the world is grey, and people are like wolves. You wake up with an aching head, hear of rumours about yourself. Your superior criticizes you unfairly. You get nothing done, wait in vain for a letter, feel old.

It's not just you and not just today. No time, no wealth, however great, no high or low position, neither cleverness nor stupidity protect people against sorrow.

The only important thing is to accept this sorrow as a cross which will save you.

21 YOU DO NOT KNOW. You stood outside a door and were sure there was going to be trouble, but you were received with open arms. You entered a house cheerfully, with a smile on your lips, and it was extinguished by indifference, disparagement or insult. You expected a reward, but no one thought of it. You were praised for something trival which you'd quite forgotten about. How often none of the possibilities you were counting on came to pass, but something happened your never thought about for a moment.

Don't put too much trust in your foresight. Reality is different. Reality is different from what you imagine. But don't be afraid of it. It comes from God.

22 LET THE DEAD BURY THEIR DEAD. Banish from your conversations questions like 'When did you take your A levels?' or 'When did you get your diploma?' as a way of quickly working out the other person's age and comparing yourself with him. Take down from the wall the pictures from years gone by, hide the album with the old photographs, put away diplomas and certificates testifying to your achievements and successes. Don't

worry, God will remember everything, but for you to remember is not only out of place but even dangerous, because it imprisons you in a world which is already past.

Feel a little pain when you remember events of the past. Stop telling stories which begin, 'In my day' or 'It was in 19—'.

Don't think I want to wipe out your past. There's enough of it in you. I just don't want you to keep on living in it. You have real tasks given you by God, the present day and the waiting future. Get on with them!

23   LET HIM NOT TURN BACK. Don't go back to places where you used to live or work, or to visit people to whom you used to be very close. Don't deceive yourself: those 'good times' will never come back. You won't find your old acquaintances again, nor will they find in you the person they once knew. For them you will be a ghost from years gone by. Their world, which once was yours, is different now, and the world you live in now is different. Each day makes you more of a stranger to them. You'll notice it in your first conversation. After the first, 'What's new with you? How are you? How are those friends of ours?' topics of conversation will dwindle. Each of you will think in embarrassment of the other, 'Hasn't he got old?'

If things turn out differently, it's proof that you've found a friend, even if you may never have called him one. But that is very rare.

24   THE BIRDS OF THE AIR. When you see something beautiful, don't reach for your camera, and don't be sorry you haven't got it with you — don't collect beautiful moments. Happiness can't be imprisoned in photograph albums, and can't be brought back by turning their pages.

Don't imagine you could never come across anything more beautiful. Go forwards. Don't worry. Reality is rich. You can't exhaust it, not even in the whole of your life.

25   LET NOT YOUR HEARTS BE TROUBLED. And when you've

convinced yourself yet again that colleagues in your field aren't keeping you informed about things which interest you so deeply, aren't asking your opinion on problems about which you have so much to say, that they are ignoring you, avoiding you, would rather you were miles away, when you've managed to convince yourself yet again that people don't like you — don't go into your empty flat on your own. Don't stay on your own. Go and see people who believe in you. Go into the presence of God. He believes in you.

26   I SAY TO YOU, RISE. God won't let you fall back into despair.
    When you're totally embittered with people, when you feel as though you're burnt out, incapable of any initiative, when you're convinced that no-one can expect anything more of you, that you no longer have the strength to do anything great, when you even lose confidence in all you've done up to now, in all your previous work, and are no longer aware of any of your positive achievements — in that situation a light will certainly shine. Someone may come up to you and say they're grateful for what you did for them, or what you were working on was very important. You may get a nice letter, or someone may smile at you.
    And this light which falls on you when you're lying in the dust like that, which brings you to your feet again, is an advance on God's judgment of your work.

27   THE TRUTH WILL MAKE YOU FREE. At least once in your life tell the truth to those who need to hear it, to those who are putting pressure on you to call black white and white black. Don't try to get out of it by telling yourself it's unimportant whether you say one thing or the other, whether you smile or nod your head. Don't say, 'They can talk. The main thing is that I know what's true'. If they try to force you to agree with the, it's because they want to humiliate you. How long can a person despise himself? And gradually you'll begin to believe that white is black and black white.

28 WHY DID YOU DOUBT? You are lost when you have no more confidence. Even if everything should go right for you. Even if people should envy you your successes.

You are secure as long as you have confidence. Even if everything keeps falling apart under your hand, even if people keep trying to destroy you. Even if you have to go against your own ego, even if the forecasts are all terrible, if defeat stares you in the face and you're terrified — as long as, with the rest of your will, you have confidence.

29 LET THE DAY'S OWN TROUBLES BE ENOUGH. You see a frail old man. You will be just like that one day. You are quite within your rights to fight against old age and illness, but it is your human duty to accept both when there is nothing more to be done, to accept them as suffering that leads to redemption. All that will come in time. Don't think about it now. Don't torment yourself unnecessarily. Trust in God: he will give you the strength to bear sufferings and the courage to accept death.

30 AT YOUR WORD I WILL LET DOWN THE NETS. Jesus is teaching on the shore. Not far away fishermen are washing their nets. The crowd of spectators grows. The master gets into one of the boats and teaches from there. When he has finished, he orders the fishermen, though they did not intend to, to put out to fish. When they return to the shore they leave everything and follow him.

For the masses a completely incomprehensible conclusion. A drama under the direction of the Son of God.

It was no accident that he came to this shore to teach. It was no accident that he has found these people there. It was no accident that he got into this boat and no other. He worked a miracle, the plentiful catch of fish. The outsiders registered something completely normal: fishermen had gone out fishing and had brought back fish. The only people who understood were Peter and his companions.

Will you be capable of understanding your life?

Bear one another's burdens

1 BLESSED ARE THOSE SERVANTS. Try to do something in life. Concentrate all your energies on this effort, subordinate the rhythm of your private affairs and your leisure to it. You may not falter, even if you see your friends piling up money. There is no risk involved, or at the most pangs of conscience on your deathbed that you didn't commit yourself totally.

Try to do something in life, no matter how old you are. There is no risk involved, or at the most pangs of conscience on your deathbed that you started too late.

If you read this and feel pleased that you are one of those to whom it has been granted to find a pearl or a treasure — I hope you may persevere with it to the end.

2 THE HARVEST HAS COME. With a great deal of effort you try to find an answer to a question that has been put to you, you cast about for a word to express what you want to say. When everyone's opinion is against you, you succeed in demonstrating the rightness of your ideas and experiences. You search feverishly for a way out of the blind alley into which your enemies have driven you, a way out of the desperate situation in which you have accidentally landed. You are on the point of finishing on time some work you have started and then come to grief on a detail, and the whole construction falls to pieces in your hands. You are weak with exhaustion, and manage to eliminate last-minute problems in a great rush. These are your great days. Then comes a period of polite smiles, calculated answers, a period when you avoid awkward subjects. You live off the interest on previously acquired capital, travel along paths you've marked out before.

But bear in mind that this is a period of rest. After a while you will again be up against a wall you must get through, at the foot of a peak which must be conquered. May your courage never fail.

3   UNLESS YOU BECOME LIKE CHILDREN. You are already fixed in your certainty that nothing else is going to happen in your life. And yet grace may touch you, and in the work you do with the apathy of a worker in a labour camp, something may fall into your hands which takes you over totally. Among the people you call by turns a flock of sheep or a pack of hyenas, you may meet one person who fascinates you. You may be shaken out of your apathy by the injury done to some defence-less person. It may happen that grace moves you and that you, whom nothing more could amaze, excite, impress or frighten, who contemplated the world with cynical tolerance, recover, just for a moment, the sensitivity of a child.

4   TO ONE HE GAVE FIVE TALENTS, TO ANOTHER TWO, TO ANOTHER ONE. Where have those nice girls gone? And those handsome boys? You can still see them, uncompromising, so simple and direct. You can still hear their sharp criticisms, their far-reaching plans, their bold ambitions. How many of them have stayed like that? And where is the vast majority? The wings have lost feathers, some teeth have gone, the people have submerged, sunk in the grey mass.

And what are you like?

As long as you have the chance of realizing your humanity, you will keep asking yourself that question.

5   TO EAT WITH UNWASHED HANDS DOES NOT DEFILE A MAN. Don't worry that much about being a person with good manners. If you make mistakes in this area, don't take them too much to heart. You might come to believe this was not the most

important thing in your life, but that is your inner honesty, the purity of your intentions, your unselfishness.

Don't worry all that much about being a person with good manners. You may come to be successful in this, and your acquaintances and you will think you are faultless — and you wouldn't even notice that inside you are a nest of serpents.

6 SHE HAS CHOSEN THE GOOD PORTION. Don't take every little thing to heart. Don't get involved in every triviality. Don't get worked up at every opportunity. Don't get annoyed whenever there's a reason. If you do, you will quite simply be absent. Absent from where you ought to be. Absent from where your vital interests are at stake.

You are not infinite, not unlimited. If you get involved in one place, you cannot be in another. It's not just your time, but your energy and your presence. So get clear about what you want to do, and concentrate on that. Otherwise you'll leave this world with the reputation of a person who was everywhere except where he was needed, busy at everything except what he was asked to do, who dreamed of a thousand things but didn't do the one thing necessary. And when someone says this to you at the end of your life, you may be appalled for the first time, because you really wanted to be quite different.

7 THE SON OF MAN MUST SUFFER. Stay. Don't run away. Prove yourself here, where you are forced into maximum concentration, precise thought, to formulate your views exactly, to vindicate your inventions, to take a position.

Stay here, where you are surrounded by enemies who check each of your steps, who mercilessly note the slightest fault, who allow no imperfection, who constantly try to trip you, to drown out your words, push you into the background, make contacts difficult for you, leave you no position of influence. They would love to get rid of you, or at least wipe out all traces of you, and so they trumpet your mistakes, broadcast your howlers, credit you with saying things you never said and attribute crimes to you which you never committed.

Hold out. Just this wood. Just this chasm, just this hill.

8 THAT YOUR JOY MAY BE FULL. Relax. Be yourself. Learn the rhythm of your personality. So that you enjoy life. That is the greatest gift God has given you — life. You are the greatest gift — your unrepeatable personality. And stay the way God made you. Tame the institutions, the people and the things which oppress you. Don't let yourself be forced into shape by the. Don't let yourself be constrained by them. Be yourself. Only then can you answer to God for this greatest of gifts — whith your happiness.

9 THE PHARISEES. Watch yourself above all when you want something from people: a job, a better job, a flat, a better flat, a loan, a grant, support and recommendation, when you want someone to sort something out for you or your family. Don't pay any price, not the price of your personal dignity, by painfully making acquaintances and keeping up unreal friendships, giving presents, writing letters, feigning friendliness, giving invitations, always saying yes and pretending admiration and enthusiasm.

You think when you've got what you're interested in, then you'll show them. You're wrong! Once you're there, you'll never find a way back again.

You'll stay a beggar always.

10 IDLE IN THE MARKET PLACE. The Lord gave you the talents. Now is your time. Have you rolled up your sleeves? Have you given everything in you that was of value? Have you already spoken your final word? Do you think you can start allowing yourself to celebrate your successes?

Now is your time. It was you the Lord gave his talents to before he went away. And he will return.

Do you at least know what you have to do in life?

11 THEY LEFT EVERYTHING. Show yourself, win standing by your presence, pretend interest and enthusiasm, but only to the extent that it doesn't commit you to anything, make promises, announce involvement, but always in a way that allows you to withdraw easily.

Shine with a couple of words tossed in, arouse interest, scheme, create uncertainty, enchant, win sympathy and love. Let others be dependent, loyal; let them worry, yearn, let them love; may their number go on increasing. In return hold out the tips of your fingers and pull them back as quickly as possible. Give nothing of yourself, to anyone. Lose nothing of yourself. Keep yourself all for you?

12 YOU CANNOT SERVE GOD AND MAMMON. While money is not involved you still don't know everything about a person. Only when there's money on the table, when it can be lost or won, only then do the crowns, the laurels and the mitres fall from the heads — or stay put. Only when money is at stake will you be able to be sure who's who. Money contains so much magic and seductiveness that it can promise you anything on earth. Only when confronted with this promise does anyone show whether he is a Christian, a believer, a human being.

13 THE RICH MAN DIED. Don't always try to work out in every situation how much they'll give you, will it pay, what will you get out of it. You can't live like that. If you are unable to love a thing or a person, really to be pleasant about something or someone, really to regret something, to be really depressed about something — you will never be able to be happy.

And when you die you'll probably have a lot of money, and perhaps you will then discover for the first time how meaningless such a life was.

14 SEEK FIRST THE KINGDOM OF GOD. It is part of our order that you should receive money — for your work, for your effort, for your commitment, for your self-sacrifice. It is part of our

125

human order that you get money for getting up in the morning, for the journey to work, for searching for truth, for your consistency, for your service to others.

But you don't work for money. You are building a world, serving other people. Don't try to shake off this yoke. Don't sell your life. Don't sell your humanity. Don't sell yourself.

15   LET US LOOK FOR A TREASURE. What are you working for? Don't try to evade this question. Don't try to push past it. Work fills your life. You devote most of your time to it, give the best hours of your days to it.

What are you working for? Look for the purpose of your work. You are, as it were, your answer to this question.

16   HE WHO HAD RECEIVED THE ONE TALENT. Work is one of the most undervalued truths. Misused, ridiculed, mocked.

You know what it's like. 'We're not that daft'. 'Who wants to work these days?' First a position, then I'll work. First a position, a desk, an official stamp, a flat, a car, first money — then I'll work. So, after incredibly complicated struggles and efforts, after nights with too little sleep, after agonized deliberation and negotiation, afer enormous effort, finally you're sitting behind this bigger desk, you've got a bigger stamp and more money. Then you'll find that you're used up, burnt out, old — incapable of anything else. And you'll feel desperately unhappy. Or not even that. Right to the end you'll go on collecting titles, official stamps, positions and money.

17   AND THEY FOLLOWED HIM. What is an ordinary day like for you? Did you really imagine your life like that? Is it as you really wanted it? What attitude do you have to your work? What do you see in it? Just the struggle for existence, positions, money, just battles with dangerous rivals? Do you also see a little love in it? No, I don't mean little politenesses, moments of honesty, generous gestures of pity performed for other people, but whether you see your work in its total meaning. Has it its source

in love or only in ambition and struggle?

18   THEY ABANDONED HIM. As long as you are carried along by human sympathy, as long as the people around you like you or get annoyed at you, expect something from you or are disturbed by you, for so long it is not clear who you really are. Only when they stop bothering with you, no longer expect anything of you and would prefer to be rid of you, when they don't notice your initiatives, show no interest in your work, when your successes leave them cold, yes when you're forced to admit the opposite, that your successes increase their animosity towards you — only then are you on the threshold of humanity. Only then can you be sure who you really are, how much you believe in yourself, in your work, in other people, in God.

19   DO NOT JUDGE BY APPEARANCES. What would you like to dress up as? As a girl or a boy, an athlete or a clown, a Mexican dancer or a sheriff, a singer with a guitar, a film star — to be able to live for one day as you'd like to live every day? But perhaps moments like that are given to you to let you see what great wealth is hidden in you, which your shyness or idleness has left unexploited.

What would you like to dress up as? As a pirate or a prostitute, a Don Juan or a gangster, a tough or a vampire — to go around for one night as you'd like to all your life. But perhaps moments like that are given to you to let you see how much evil, how much brutality, quarrelsomeness and nastiness are dormant in you which have not yet come to the surface because of your shyness, your idleness or lack of opportunity.

20   BUT HE WHO ENDURES TO THE END WILL BE SAVED. It's easy to work, it's easy to be kind when someone notices it, accepts it and is pleased. When our actions receive the approval of our neightbours, when we are praised and honoured. When this activity of ours is regarded by everyone as a success.

It is difficult to work when no one sees us, when no one can appreciate the trouble, self-sacrifice, effort we put in every day. When we seem to go on living in a vacuum, in oblivion.

But it is even harder to work when people turn away from us even though we give everything in our power. When we are confronted by a lack of trust, disapproval and reproach, no longer just indifference, but hostility. To work and give oneself then, to be kind and to endure then — that is what being human means.

21 WHERE YOUR TREASURE IS. Suppose you were suddenly to lose everything you have, everything you've taken such pains to earn, gather together, save, acquire, grab, invest safely and put aside.

Suppose you were suddenly to lose all that. Would your only salvation and consolation be the certainty — or at least the quiet hope — that you would still be capable of making good these losses, that you were still strong, nifty, fly, prudent, and by now experienced and clever enough to get back what you'd lost, and maybe to acquire even more than you possessed before?

What is the meaning of your life?

22 BUT HE WAS ASLEEP. Jesus knew that he only had three years to communicate his truth to men. He began at the age of thirty. After forty days of fasting in the wilderness. And later too he often withdrew, with his disciples or alone, from the work of preaching. As well, he limited his activity just to Palestine.

As well as cancer and heart disease, mental illness is becoming a major threat to society. One reason for this threat is inability to make time to rest. We are exhausted by the monotony of our jobs, by the labyrinth of city life, the activity, the restaurants, the crowds of people, the rush-hour traffic, the noise in the streets and at home.

This is why you should insert into the rhythm of your work a rhythm of rest, a longish period of relaxation once a year, a shorter one each week, a break every day. You've no time? Go on holiday anyway. Still go for a walk, to a concert, to see friends. Spend the evening with a book or a magazine.

If you don't you won't be able to cope with everything. Have a good rest; you're not irreplaceable. Have a good rest. If you don't want to, and insist on carrying on as you are you're already in a very bad way.

23   THE SONS OF THIS WORLD. When you're almost in danger of suffocating, when they hem you in even tighter with their pleas, with their pressure and their demands; when they try to force you to listen endlessly to their worries, when they terrorize you with their petty problems in an effort to force you to do even the simplest things for them, and it then turns out that your help wasn't necessary at all, and with a slight effort they could have managed themselves; when they cheerfully take up whole hours of your time while you go frantic over each wasted minute, and at the same time react with amazement to the slightest request from you, either forget it or simply reject it; when you see that they don't think at all about your responsibilities or resources, and are only looking for their own comfort; when you have no time for your own affairs, neglect your responsibilities and rush around from morning till night, go away from them quickly. You — all of you, you and they — have lost a sense of proportion and your behaviour has lost all connection with love.

24   REST A LITTLE. You feel as though your hands are dropping off. You're convinced that your work is not only boring but totally meaningless. You see clearly how people exploit you. You are profoundly disappointed, not only in your colleagues but also in your friends, and you're beginning to believe you can't rely on anyone but yourself. You tell yourself you've at least seen the world as it really is. You need a rest, the longer and more complete the more you think you've at last seen the truth.

    And if you can't leave your post at any price, at least take a breather. Go to the theatre, to the cinema. Pick up a book, go for a walk or step into a church for a minute.

25   WISE AS SERPENTS. Learn to say no. Learn not to say things. Don't lose control over the time you give to others.

Otherwise people will take your life out of your hands, destroy your rhythm, stop you from carrying out your plans and absorb you in their affairs. And when you can be no more use to them, they'll throw you away. Then it may already be too late for you to put your life together again.

Learn to refuse your help occasionally. Against all appearances, that is often more difficult than saying yes. Learn to say no — unless you do that very well already.

26 LAZARUS, COME OUT. Are you able to enjoy life, getting up, eating, going to work, work itself, going home, rest, sleep, the rough surface of a wall, the brilliance of snow, the blue of the sky, the struggle, even if it ends in defeat? Even sometimes? Or are you only left with the tiredness, exhaustion to the point of nausea — the lot of the slave, who falls on to his bed in the evening as he will one day fall into his grave?

You know, life is the greatest gift God could have given you.

27 FEAR NOT, LITTLE FLOCK. You'll die a year or maybe ten years too early. Of a heart attack. You get agitated to the limit of toleration by the insult some stranger calls after you in the street, it annoys you when people slam doors, a rumour spread about you hurts.

You'll die too early. You get irritated to death because someone pushes in front of you in the queue, because someone doesn't return money he borrowed from you, because someone brushes against you in the street without apologizing, because you have paid a fine undeservedly.

You'll die too early and not complete what you might have done — energies you need for important things will fail. All because you haven't learn to dismiss as unimportant things which are unimportant.

28 HE SETTLED ACCOUNTS WITH THEM. We get ill too often, we get old too early, our lives are too short. We don't know how to work, how to relax — we don't know how to live. We are

130

superficial and haste in eating and drinking. We use our energy badly, we manage our time badly, we apportion our day badly. We squander our energies. We imagine that they come from an inexhaustible spring. We waste them on trivia, we exhaust them by getting excessively irritated about something, making ourselves rush; we get excited and get worried for no reason.

Until it hits us like a blow. Then it's hard for us to believe that it's already too late, that we have no reserves left, that the changes can no longer be reversed, the processes are too far advanced, that life is indeed already over.

We get ill too often, we get old too early, our lives are too short.

29   YOU ARE ANXIOUS AND TROUBLED ABOUT MANY THINGS. You are increasingly pressurized, run off your feet, you get busier and busier. More and more you lose yourself. More and more often you stop being you. You are no more than a creature driven by outside impulses, with only the instinct for self-defence left, a thrashing of elbows which enables you to keep yourself on the surface.

Sometimes grace hits you in the face like a wet branch. You are appalled at yourself: 'What has happened to me? What his life done to me?' Sometimes grace hits you like a wet branch – and you come to your senses and save yourself. But sometimes not even grace can help you any more.

30   BLESSED ARE THE MERCIFUL. You must help the other person when he loses his way, gets entangled in the labyrinth of a strange life, when he is not able to sort out his affairs. You must help him to overcome his crisis and draw breath.

But be careful. At the same time you start getting him used to always relying on your help. You begin to justify his confusion. To get him used to looking round for someone else's compassion. And your next step is not love; it demoralizes him. You teach him idleness, passivity, an easy life, cunning.

31 LET HIM TAKE UP HIS CROSS. Somewhere in the darkness of uncertainty there is still inside you a glimmer of hope that your skill in living and protecting yourself will preserve you from serious illnesses and a frail old age.

Somewhere in the darkness of uncertainty there is still inside you a glimmer of hope that your knowledge of the world will protect you against the harm people may try and do to you.

And although you are going through a waterless waste, although you are spared nothing and given nothing — somewhere in the darkness of uncertainty there is still a glimmer of hope inside you.

You will find rest

1   DO NOT LAY UP FOR YOURSELVES TREASURES ON EARTH. If there is something that the rest of us really envy — to the point of hate — it's life. And if we are really afraid of anything it's death. And in this fear you cram your prockets to overflowing, stuff your belly full, collect things in pigeon-holes, drawers and cupboards, entrench yourself around yourself. It gets harder and harder for you to give anything away; you skimp on everything and gather around you people who might be useful to you in bad times.

    Is this a way of protecting yourself against death?

2   ON EARTH. We save, collect and stuff every corner with supplies. We choose what is the most lasting and the best value. We look for what pays best. We calculate what we can make most on, what we can sell off at the highest price. We are worried about not making a loss and winning as much as possible, never losing but always being on the winning side. We struggle to defend what we've accumulated, and hold on to what we've won.

    How many sleepless nights are written off to such calculations? How much wasted time goes on such considerations! How much life lost!

3   WHILE YOU HAVE THE LIGHT. Don't put if off. Get a move on. Do what you have to do. Say what you have to say. The

shadow is already moving forwards, and will soon have absorbed you. And you will be left with the after-taste of an unfulfilled life. Or not even that. An old person's satisfaction over a bowl of soup you didn't let anyone else take away from you right to the end.

4　HE WENT AWAY, FOR HE HAD GREAT POSSESSIONS. There is no irritation, no injury, no misfortune, which could be a total catastrophe for you. That would only be possible if you lived on earth for ever. But how many years have you got in front of you? Ten, twenty, fifty? Certainly not more. And that only if everything goes well.

There is no success, no wealth, no money that can guarantee you lasting happiness. That would be conceivable only if you lived on earth for ever. But how many more years will you live? Maybe fifty, maybe ten, and then only if everything runs its normal course.

Right to the end, to the last breath, you nourish within you the hope that you will be an exception. And so death will get you in mid-stride. You will meet it with great amazement.

5　AND THE MOON WILL NOT GIVE ITS LIGHT. We are approaching the summits of our civilization, and can already imagine its end. Even if we do not die from the consequences of a nuclear disaster, we will die of a lack of coal, oil or iron, poisoned by our food, suffocated by atmospheric pollution or exhaust fumes, we will freeze to death or evaporate in the heat.

And although we must go on building factories, motorways and mines, we see clearly as never before that all this has no value in itself; it is not our final goal.

6　LET YOUR LIGHT SO SHINE BEFORE MEN. In the course of the years you become like a flag, made more and more tattered by squalls, a tree at a cross-roads bent by the wind, cracked by the frost, dried up by the heat, a wall scarred by shots. Until the next shock comes, the next tug, the storm that throws you to the ground.

If only you can go on to the end with head held high. If only you can be like a torch, showing people the way.

7   HE WHO BELIEVES IN ME SHALL LIVE. There comes a moment when you see your shadow. From that point it is your constant companion. You acquire knowledge. When an illness occurs, you ask yourself, 'Have things gone that far?' And when disabilities appear, you ask yourself, 'Have things gone that far?' But even if your answer is, 'No, not yet', your smile still doesn't mean a complete victory. You know death will get you.

We have knowledge. We come closer and closer to those who were with us only a short time ago. The ties we feel with them are also getting closer.

8   THERE HE SQUANDERED HIS PROPERTY. Somehow life has rushed on. Before you realized it, you were no longer a child. Before you realized it, you had stopped being a young man or a young woman — you were a mature person. And so life rushed past you. Inside you the question presses harder and harder: 'Is all that really in the past?' Of course you keep on promising yourself, 'When I've got to the most important things done, I'll start to enjoy life. I'll go to the theatre, to a concert, have a holiday, and sort out my affairs with God'.

That's completely the wrong way round. You ought to enjoy your everyday life. Each thing you do should link you to God.

9   LIKE TRAVELLERS. You imagine that it will be like all those other times you set off on a long journey. You quickly sort out your last affairs — they'd been waiting around for ages — you leave behind last instructions. Once more your friends and colleagues are tested. In the last few hours they show themselves to be calculating, insulted or sympathetic, tolerant and absolutely loyal. Once more you'll say to each of them, 'Excuse all that irritability, excuse this rush. Say goodbye to your sister for me, say goodbye to your father. Goodbye — yes, see you again'. A

135

last smile, a last handshake, a last look at the people who have accompanied you through life. A last sigh, and a last tear rolls over your face.

And yet it will still come as a surprise. You won't know, right to the end, that things have gone so far.

10   SEEK. Don't say you're a progressive, and don't say that you're not a progressive. Don't say you're a conservative, or that you're not a conservative. Don't say you're an intellectual. Don't say you're an expert.

Don't say that everything in the past was good, and don't say that everything in the past was bad. Don't say that everything new is good or that everything new is bad.

Why are you becoming rigid? Be free. Stay open, fresh, prepared. Don't be afraid, or you'll be easy to bowl over, finish off, destroy. Don't be afraid of anything at all.

11   BUT DELIVER US FROM THE EVIL ONE. We don't need to be afraid of death. It will mean that we transcend, one more time, fear about our own life and our own future, one more time worry about our own comfort. That one more time we go out beyond ourselves, as we do with every victory over self, every act of unselfish help, every commitment to another person or to society, every piece of honest work. It will be one more step towards love.

12   WALK WHILE YOU HAVE THE LIGHT. While you have supple hands, while your feet will carry you, while you can think logically, while you can work up enthusiasm for something . . . .

For later a time will come when you won't even be capable of that, even if you wanted to. For later a time may come when you aren't even capable of wanting it any more, and you're left just with fear about preserving your troublesome existence.

13   YOUR FATHER IN HEAVEN. One more piece of bread, one

more swallow of water, one more heart attack. One more day, one more night, fine weather, rain, a breath of wind, a snowflake.

One more pleasure, sadness or moment of exhaustion, a period of relaxation, kindness, an unpleasantness, an excitement, a disappointment, a pleasure, a time of loneliness.

How does one give thanks?

14 AT AN HOUR WHEN YOU DO NOT EXPECT. It's no time to die in spring, when everything around you is green.

It's no time to die when you are in the fulness of your creative forces — in the summer of your life.

It's no time to die when you can finally enjoy the fruits of your labour.

Is it time to die?

15 YOUR DAYS. Afterwards there will be silence. And cold ashes. But now you are still burning. You still glow and shoot out streams of sparks. Sometimes you go rather quiet, but then you flare up again. You give off heat. People gather round you. They contemplate the miracle of your personality. They warm their hands at it. Often they don't know whether the warmth is love or passion, courage or vanity, kindness or fear. But you yourself need to know. You must keep on asking yourself what it is that's burning in you, courage or vanity, love or passion, kindness or fear?

Soon, you know, you'll go out. Then he will come and look in your ashes to see if anything is left of your life.

16 AT THAT TIME. All that will be left of you will be a pair of worn shoes, some old clothes, a few bills and notes that no one feels like reading. Someone will look at all that and say, 'Well, not much left of him'.

But when you look at the 'little' that is left of a human being who was close to you, you know that that's not true; no, he stands before God just as he was day by day all his life.

17 AS YOU DID IT TO ONE OF THE LEAST OF THESE MY BRETHREN, YOU DID IT TO ME. You won't be asked then whether you were baptized, whether you wore a cassock or a habit, a roll-neck sweater or a tie, whether you had a master's or a doctor's degree, whether you had the keys of the kingdom or the key of the door. What you'll be asked then is whether you were a human being.

18 LET NOT YOUR HEARTS BE TROUBLED. You need to straighten the wooden cross in the cemetery, because it's a bit crooked. You must cut the shrubs and loosen the earth. In the coming year you may put up a stone, but first the earth has to settle. For the moment you just plant two chrysanthemums.

And then you let your hands drop. What's it all for? Is it a sort of clasp round the dead person to fold up her life neatly. You know her. You remember the way she talked, her ideas, intentions and plans. Death intervened and tore everything to pieces.

You go through the cemetery. From time to time you come across names you know. You think of the people who have gone. Young people, old people.

Simplest perhaps is the death of a small child. It doesn't know anything yet. It hasn't yet been able to get deeply fond of anything. The more years go by, the more people realize their possibilities, whole worlds open in front of them, and they begin to understand their task. And then they have to go.

Can human life be complete without eternal life?

19 WHOM THE MASTER FINDS AWAKE WHEN HE COMES. We stand in front of their graves, lay wreaths and flowers, light candles. We contemplate their lives — with which our own was intertwined — their joys, worries, hours of distress, their work, their successes and moments of inspiration, their failures, their mistakes, their breakdowns. But now, already, there is silence. They have finished their race. We need no longer fear for them, or make ourselves anxious and upset. They are in the hand of the merciful Father.

We go away from their graves, relieved about them, but increasingly disturbed about ourselves and our neighbours.

20 I WILL NOT LEAVE YOU DESOLATE. Dead relatives frequently appear to me in dreams, mother, father, brother. Sometimes they are sad, sometimes happy. They say something. I wake up — and I can still hear their voices. Sometimes they leave behind a feeling of peace, sometimes fear.

Our relatives are close to us. How much stronger than before is their presence. Now they are no longer just here or there; now they are always with us.

We visit their graves, put flowers on them and light candles — signs of remembrance, gratitude and love. But the true sign of our remembrance, gratitude and love can only be our daily lives, which go on in their sight.

21 IF THE GRAINS DIES. No, don't look for suffering, not for defeats, failures, humiliations. Don't pray for them. But do realize that their presence in your life is something normal, indeed essential. Granted, while you are suffering you can't say this. Then there's only suffering, though even then, deep in your mind there must be the conviction that's quite proper. After all, only when you meet resistance do you gird yourself for the struggle.

The greatest temptation which threatens you is that of going through life peacefully. Not coming into conflict with people on the left or people on the right, with those above you or those below you, with those near you or those at a distance. If you had two lives you could allow yourself to take one life easy. But you only have one. You only get one chance to judge everything in the truth, to say everything you think, to say yes and no, to do everything you want — to become a human being. You only get a chance like that once.

22 IT IS FINISHED. And what about when it's your turn to die on the cross? To die in the knowledge that you didn't get rich, that you didn't get a great position or make a name for yourself. What about when it's your turn to die on the cross, lonely and abandoned?

What sort of life will you regard as wasted, squandered, thrown away? What do you want? What are you interested in in life? What do you regard as valuable? What would you like? Find an answer before it's your turn to die on the cross.

23 PUT OUT YOUR HAND AND PLACE IT IN MY SIDE. All we take with us into that other world is our cross, the constant struggle to break through our egoism, our indifference, idleness and fear.

Only our cross can take us into that other world.

24 IF ANY MAN WOULD COME AFTER ME. There will be a cross over your grave. Will it be the most accurate symbol of your life? Or only an accident? Or a misunderstanding?

You still have your time. You still have your life. You are still being asked questions, still being answered, still making decisions. You are still faced with your responsibilities at work, you still face your enemies. Is the cross the most accurate symbol of this life?

25 TODAY YOU WILL BE WITH ME IN PARADISE. Tell yourself you're going to live as though this was the last year of your life. No, not 'as though'; tell yourself it is the last year of your life. And if at the end of this year you tell me — though I may not be still there — with a certain satisfaction, 'But it wasn't the last year of my life', you haven't lost anything. You can only live authentically if you give your life ultimate dimensions. Only then can you decide properly, work properly, speak properly and think properly. After all, it may really be the last year of your life.

26 LET THE DEAD BURY THEIR DEAD. My wish for you in the

last night of the year is that — no matter how many years you have behind you — you may not be old. That you won't dig out your medals and decorations, even on special occasions, that you won't puff yourself up by remembering old times, the good old days, the good years, that you won't dilute the gifts God has given you over coffee cups, in repeating rumours, in trying to work out how much this one earns or what that one's health's like.

27 HE WHO BELIEVES IN ME. If there was a water of life in the world, to get it we would go through seven rivers, over seven mountains, through seven woods and seven seas. If we could obtain the water of life, no sacrifice, no effort, no price would be too high for us to pay ... If someone promised us the water of life, there is no one to whom we would be more grateful. Water of life. Eternal life.

28 WE BRING YOU TIDINGS OF GREAT JOY. Were you really brought tidings of great joy? Are you glad you believed in Jesus, glad you are a Christian? Do you feel faith is a valuable gift? Is it for you a treasure found, the pearl of great price? Are you happy?

29 WHO WAIT FOR THEIR LORD. How does one live between heaven and earth? Why should we struggle for every breath, through the next heart attack, if eternal life is really waiting for us? Why build up what will be destroyed? Why accumulate what will be scattered? Why settle when you'll immediately have to get up and go on?

How does one live between earth and eternity? What ground rules can we find in the struggle for every hour of our life? In the end we must build up, even if it will be destroyed, we must collect things even if they will subsequently be scattered. Only don't settle comfortably. You will soon have to get up and go on.

30 HE WHO HAD RECEIVED THE FIVE TALENTS. The game's over. Count the cards. How did you do? Count up. What were the past months like? Difficult? Did you do a lot of work? Did you achieve much? Maybe you just got through, just coped somehow, and now, when you look back, you just see a blur.

But the cards have been dealt again. The game's starting. You don't know what else you may pick up during the game. But you're on your own in the game. Are you better at it than you were in the past few months? Have your set-backs, your defeats, and your successes and achievements, made you wise? Do you know now what life is about?